DR. TRYPHENA RUTH BANKS

BRIDGING THE GAP

A SURVIVOR S GUIDE TO THE GEN JUNGLE

BRIDGING
THE GAP

A SURVIVOR'S GUIDE TO THE GEN JUNGLE

DR. TRYPHENA RUTH BANKS

CITI OF
BOOKS

CITIOFBOOKS, INC.
3736 Eubank NE Suite A1
Albuquerque, NM 87111-3579
www.citiofbooks.com
Hotline: 1 (877) 389-2759
Fax: 1 (505) 930-7244

Ordering Information:

Quantity sales. Special discounts are available on quantity purchases by corporations, associations, and others. For details, contact the publisher at the address above.

Printed in the United States of America.

ISBN-13:   Paperback   979-8-89391-765-9
                      eBook   979-8-89391-767-3

Library of Congress Control Number: 2025912592

TABLE OF CONTENTS

— DEDICATION —

To my family—across generations, from the Silent Generation, Baby Boomers, and Generation X, to Millennials, Generation Z, and Generation Alpha.

Thank you for your unique contributions. The lessons I've learned from each of you are invaluable, and your presence in my life is deeply cherished.

— Acknowledgments —

I extend my deepest gratitude to all generations, past and present. Your invaluable contributions to society have shaped our world in countless ways, and your legacies inspire us all. Thank you for being an essential part of this ever-evolving journey we share.

To my beloved sisters Ophelia Sanders and Schola Innocent—your unwavering belief in me and constant encouragement have been a guiding light throughout this book-writing journey. I am profoundly grateful for your support and friendship.

— ABOUT THE AUTHOR —

Dr. Tryphena Ruth Banks is a dedicated Registered Professional Nurse from Liberia, West Africa, with a diverse heritage of Bassa, Dan, and Gola descent. As a mother of four and grandmother of eight, spanning generations from millennials to Gen Alpha, she brings a wealth of lived experience and a distinctive multicultural perspective to her work. Dr. Banks holds a Master's degree in Nursing Education and a Doctorate in Healthcare Administration. Her career has been dedicated to serving individuals across a wide spectrum of ages, cultures, and beliefs, reflecting her passion for fostering collaboration, respect, and effective communication. Dr. Banks's commitment to these values is evident in her efforts to strengthen personal and professional relationships, ultimately contributing to a more peaceful and harmonious society.

— PREFACE —

Bridging the Gap celebrates the diverse perspectives that define our world, from the stoic wisdom of the Silent Generation to the rebellious spirit of the Baby Boomers, the pragmatic insights of Gen X, the tech-savvy approach of Gen Z, and the digitally native mindset of Generation Alpha. This book emphasizes that our world is a vibrant tapestry woven with similarities and differences across generations. By cultivating patience and respect, we can build stronger relationships, enhance communication, and create a more harmonious community where we learn from and appreciate one another, regardless of our generational backgrounds. Ultimately, we are all branches of the same tree, striving for a better world, with each generation contributing a unique melody to the timeless symphony of life.

— Introduction —

People adapt to their environments and share the traits of their ancestors, which were passed on to them biologically and socially. That is to say, knowledge is accumulative and ever-evolving. Quoting Mannheim here would be essential to understand how different generations are unique due to their socioeconomic and political conditions and why they need one another in this new, highly complex, and advanced world. This book underscores that the concept of a generation is not merely about chronological age but about shared experiences and collective responses.

Sociological research suggests generations are social phenomena shaped by the interaction between individual biographies and broader historical processes. This perspective shifts the focus from individual aging to the collective dynamics of generational cohorts. It illustrates that generational identity is forged through personal experiences and societal conditions.

Here is an example to analyze how different generations function and how they differ regarding social mores and norms, how they see work-life balance, and the rapid shift in their value systems.

Scenario: Generational Clash in a High-Stakes Workplace Project

Imagine a setting where five different generations are present working on the same project:

A multinational tech company is launching a critical project to develop an innovative AI-driven product. The project team consists of members from five generations: The Silent Generation, Baby Boomers, Generation X, Millennials, and Generation Z.

There are five team members from the above-mentioned generations.

Elizabeth (Silent Generation, born 1938): Who is a seasoned consultant brought in for her extensive experience in crisis management and corporate strategy.

Fredrick (Baby Boomer, born 1955) has been assigned as a project manager. He has a wealth of knowledge in traditional project management and a hierarchical approach to leadership.

Sheron (Generation X, born 1970): She's a senior developer who values independence and prefers practical problem-solving methods and work-life balance.

Michael (Millennial, born 1985): He's a tech-savvy marketer enthusiastic about innovation and collaboration. He's always motivated by a strong sense of purpose and social responsibility.

Jacob (Generation Z, born 2000): He's a junior developer adept at using the latest digital tools. He prefers fast communication and a flexible work environment.

The first day of the meeting:

Elizabeth (Silent Generation) starts the meeting by emphasizing the importance of a structured, methodical approach to the project. She draws on historical precedents and stresses the value of meticulous planning and risk management.

Fredrick (Baby Boomer) supports Elizabeth's perspective, but he adds a layer of traditional project management techniques. He advocates for clear hierarchies and defined roles and responsibilities within the team, believing that a top-down approach will ensure accountability and efficiency.

However, Sheron (Generation X) voices her preference for a more flexible and autonomous working environment. She believes in the importance of balancing work and personal life and suggests that the team should allow for remote work and flexible hours to boost productivity and morale.

Michael (Millennial) challenges the traditional views. He wants to promote a collaborative way of handling things. He also highlights the need for cross-functional teams and feedback at every stage to continue forward with a proper vision and focus on the project's social impact. Michael also suggests leveraging social media and digital platforms for marketing and customer engagement.

Jacob (Generation Z), the youngest team member, wants to incorporate the latest digital tools at their disposal and agile methodologies. His approach is tech-savvy, and he believes that digital tools can enhance the quality of the overall project and make it more efficient. Real-time communication via instant messaging apps and a more informal, inclusive working environment are essential and conducive for everyone.

Analyzing the parts where Clash and Collaboration occur:

So, the first meeting reveals stark differences in the perspectives and value systems of these five different generations. Elizabeth and Fredrick feel the need for a more controlled and hierarchical approach, while Sheron, Michael, and Jacob push for flexibility, collaboration, and the use of cutting-edge technologies.

The points of contention among these five generations:

Regarding planning and strategy, Elizabeth and Fredrick both favor long-term planning and require detailed documentation regarding the project, while Sheron, Michael, and Jacob prefer quick methods that use technological solutions and promote adaptability.

In the area of communication, Elizabeth and Fredrick rely mostly on formal emails and scheduled meetings. In contrast, Sheron prefers a mix of email and face-to-face discussions, while Michael and Jacob advocate for instant messaging and virtual collaboration.

These different generations prefer somewhat different work environments. For instance, the older generations prefer a structured office environment, while the younger generations push for remote work options and flexible hours that create a sense of work-life balance.

Nevertheless, the question is, how do we progress when considering that these five generations have to work together on this project?

To move forward, the team decides to integrate the strengths of each generation:

From Elizabeth to Fredrick: They decide to go with a foundational strategy with clear objectives and risk management protocols. This provides a stable framework within which the team can operate.

From Sheron: They incorporate flexible working hours with the option of remote working so as not to disturb their healthy work-life balance.

From Michael: The project embraces a collaborative approach, with regular feedback loops and a focus on the project's wider social impact.

From Jacob: The team applies the latest digital tools for communication and project management, which fosters a more vigorous and responsive work environment.

Despite the apparent differences in outlooks and value systems across generations, all generations are, indeed, riding the same rollercoaster of human experience. They face universal challenges and share common dreams and threats. The crucial task is learning how to navigate these modern challenges together and finding creative ways to address problems that can improve life for everyone.

This book will shed light on the universal challenges that are faced by these different generations, technological changes over the decades, the issues of globalization, and the existential threat of climate change, and how they have been navigating through those challenges so far and where work needs to be done still.

Appreciating the historical and social contexts that shape generational views, value systems, and social mores can lead to more effective communication and reduced intergenerational conflict.

The interplay of generational differences is a potent force shaping the modern world. By embracing these differences and leveraging the strengths of each generation, People can drive progress and create a more cohesive and dynamic society. To navigate these modern challenges effectively, fostering intergenerational collaboration and leveraging each age group's unique strengths is crucial.

— Part I —
TIME TRAVELERS' DIARIES

— Chapter 1 —
BLAST FROM THE PAST - THE OG GENERATIONS

As with all generations, the birth years assigned to the Silent Generation can differ based on who is defining the term. However, they are commonly recognized by the dates ranging from 1928 to 1945. These years cover the period from the start of the Great Depression to the end of World War II. Individuals born during this time are sometimes also referred to as "Radio Babies" or "Traditionalists."

The "silent" nature of this generation is often linked to the challenging circumstances of their birth and their coming of age during the era of McCarthyism. Although the Silent Generation is characterized by traditionalist behavior and a preference for working within the system rather than challenging it, many outspoken and unconventional members of this generation made significant contributions to shaping the world we live in today.

This generation faced adversities unlike others and endured lasting mental traumas due to political and economic upheaval during that time. Wars, starvation, and the looming threat of total annihilation remained their reality for a long time.

This generation faced an acute shortage of life-sustaining resources. Events like the Great Depression exacerbated the existing problems in many societies worldwide. The Great Depression was marked by extreme economic hardship, widespread unemployment, famines in the south of the United States, and poverty. Many families struggled to make ends meet, facing food shortages, loss of homes, and a general lack of financial security. This environment of scarcity taught the Silent Generation the importance of conserving resources and avoiding waste.

Hence, this generation adopted habits that were shaped by their social settings. The history and the socio-political changes during that time shaped their habits and behaviors. Following are some of the habits that were acquired by this particular generation.

Growing up in a time when every penny counted, members of the Silent Generation learned to be thrifty. They learned to live with less and what they had available during the hard times. They repaired and reused items rather than discarding them. This habit of frugality became deeply ingrained, influencing their financial decisions throughout their lives.

The economic instability of their childhood led the Silent Generation to prioritize saving money over spending it. They valued financial security and were cautious about taking on debt, preferring to save for future needs and emergencies. They had a conservative mindset when it came to investing money. They often preferred stable, low-risk options like government bonds and savings accounts over more volatile investments like stocks.

The shared sense of sacrifice is also a prominent feature of this generation. World War II demanded significant sacrifices from civilians and soldiers alike. The war effort required everyone to contribute through rationing, buying war bonds, or working in war-related industries. This sense of collective duty and nationalism reinforced the values of hard work and dedication among the young.

Their work ethic was solely a byproduct of their social settings. The ongoing wars urged them to develop highly organized military-industrial complexes and required every citizen to participate somehow. Many members of the Silent Generation either served in the military or worked in these industries, supporting their country's war efforts. These experiences instilled discipline, punctuality, and a strong work ethic. The rigorous demands of military service and industrial production highlighted the value of perseverance and hard work.

After the war, there was a strong emphasis on rebuilding economies and societies. The Silent Generation was integral to the post-war economic boom, taking on roles in emerging industries and contributing to significant economic growth. Their willingness to work long hours and commit to their jobs was crucial in this period of reconstruction and prosperity.

After analyzing the factors behind the silent generation's way of seeing society in a particular way, it is time to shed light on another essential generation that shaped the world after the war ended: the Boomer generation.

A Baby Boomer is a member of the generation born during the post-World War II baby boom in the United States and other countries. The sheer size of this generation in the U.S., coupled with technological advancements and geopolitical factors, significantly transformed the nation politically, culturally, and economically.

The Baby Boomers, born approximately between 1946 and 1964, underwent a remarkable and transformative journey that profoundly shaped their collective identity as a generation. In their youth, they were deeply immersed in countercultural movements that championed radical change, social justice, and a rejection of traditional norms. The "flower power" ethos epitomized their desire for peace, love, and harmony, and their activism challenged the established social and political order, leaving an indelible mark on society. Unlike their predecessor (the silent generation), this generation decided to speak up against the wrongs that plagued their societies. This period of their lives was characterized by a profound sense of idealism, a passion for social justice, and a commitment to creating a more equitable and compassionate world.

While the Baby Boomer generation is frequently defined by the iconic moments of their teenage years—such as the embrace of hippie culture, widespread protests against the Vietnam War in the 1960s-1970s, and the legendary 1969 Woodstock concert—it was during the 1980s that they began to wield substantial economic and political power. This shift marked a significant transition from their youth's rebellious and idealistic values to a more pragmatic and ambitious focus on professional and financial success. As they entered their prime working years, this generation brought with them the innovative spirit and drive that characterized their early experiences, profoundly influencing various aspects of society.

By the 1980s, most of the American workforce was comprised of Baby Boomers, many of whom were ascending the corporate ladder or pioneering new ventures. This era saw Boomers stepping into leadership roles, leveraging their unique blend of idealism and pragmatism to reshape the business landscape. Prominent figures from this generation, such as

Steve Jobs and Steve Wozniak, who co-founded Apple, and Bill Gates, who co-founded Microsoft, exemplify the entrepreneurial zeal that drove the technological revolution. These innovators were instrumental in creating entirely new industries, revolutionizing technology, and transforming the economy. Their contributions propelled economic growth and set the stage for the digital age, highlighting the significant impact of Baby Boomers on shaping modern society.

During the Baby Boomer generation, the political landscape underwent significant changes driven by major historical events such as the Cold War, the Civil Rights Movement, and the Moon Landing. The Cold War, characterized by intense rivalry between the United States and the Soviet Union, fostered a climate of fear and suspicion but also a sense of national unity and purpose. The threat of nuclear war and the push for technological and military superiority influenced Boomers to value strong national defense, patriotism, and innovation. This period saw significant government investment in science and technology, culminating in the Space Race and the Moon Landing in 1969, which not only represented a triumph of human ingenuity but also reinforced the values of perseverance, ambition, and American exceptionalism.

The Civil Rights Movement of the 1950s and 1960s profoundly shaped this generation's social and political values. Witnessing and participating in the struggle for racial equality instilled a strong sense of justice and activism in them. The movement's successes, including landmark legislation like the Civil Rights Act of 1964 and the Voting Rights Act of 1965, highlighted the importance of civic engagement and the power of collective action. This era also saw the rise of other social movements, such as feminism and environmentalism, further shaping Boomers' commitment to equality, social justice, and the protection of natural resources. These historical events collectively influenced the Baby Boomers to prioritize both national strength and social progress, creating a complex and multifaceted political identity.

During this period, Baby Boomers exerted significant cultural influence. The television show "Thirtysomething," which debuted in 1987, coincided with the 30th anniversary of the peak Baby Boomer birth year in 1957. This era also saw the creation of a Baby Boomer edition of the popular board game Trivial Pursuit and the release of the film "Baby Boom" in

1987. Steven Spielberg, one of the most celebrated filmmakers of the decade, was born in the inaugural year of the Baby Boom. Oprah Winfrey, who was born in 1954, launched her nationally syndicated talk show in 1986, quickly becoming a cultural icon. Additionally, music icons Michael Jackson and Madonna, both born in 1958, produced some of the most defining music of the era.

This generation experienced a profound musical evolution, transitioning from jazz and rock 'n' roll to disco, reflecting and shaping their time's societal changes and youth culture. With its roots in African American culture and its improvisational complexity, jazz resonated with Boomers in their early years, symbolizing freedom and intellectual sophistication. The rise of rock 'n' roll in the 1950s and 1960s marked a pivotal shift, with its raw energy and rebellious themes echoing this generation's desire to break free from conservative norms. Icons like Elvis Presley and Chuck Berry provided a soundtrack for the civil rights movement and youth defiance, integrating social consciousness with musical innovation.

By the mid-1970s, the emergence of disco brought a new wave of cultural influence. Disco's infectious beats and dance rhythms, popularized by artists like Donna Summer and the Bee Gees, reflected the era's social liberation and celebration of diversity. The rise of disco clubs offered Boomers spaces for free expression and inclusivity, mirroring the growing acceptance of diverse lifestyles, including the LGBTQ+ community. Disco's emphasis on fun and escapism provided a counterbalance to the economic uncertainties of the time, while its electronic production techniques heralded the future of music. This musical journey, from jazz and rock 'n' roll to disco, encapsulates the dynamic interplay between music and the evolving societal landscape of the Boomer generation.

In the upcoming chapter, Gen X will navigate a world profoundly shaped by the preceding Baby Boomer generation, grappling with shifting values and behaviors in an increasingly uncertain global landscape. As they inherit Boomers' cultural and economic legacies, Gen Xers will likely confront unique challenges and opportunities influenced by rapid technological advancements, evolving social norms, and the lingering impacts of previous generations' decisions.

— Chapter 2 —
Gen X - The Original Rebels

Generation X refers to the cohort of Americans born between 1965 and 1980, though exact birth years may vary slightly across different sources. Often dubbed the "middle child" generation, Generation X sits between the prominent baby boomers and the millennials (Generation Y). Another nickname that is often used for this group is the "baby bust" generation, mainly due to the significant drop in birth rates following the baby boom era, partly influenced by the advent of the birth control pill in the early 1960s. Consequently, this particular generation is also smaller than the preceding baby boomers, the subsequent millennials, and Generation Z (those born between 1997 and the early 2010s). This smaller population size is a key factor in why Generation X is sometimes perceived as being overlooked or forgotten in discussions about generational differences.

Generation X is often referred to as the "latchkey kid" generation because they grew up during a time when dual-income households and rising divorce rates became more common. As a result, many Gen X children came home from school to empty houses, with house keys often tied around their necks. This independence was a necessity and a defining characteristic of their upbringing. Without parents' constant supervision, these children learned to take care of themselves, manage household chores, and navigate their free time without guidance. This early experience of self-sufficiency fostered a strong sense of autonomy and resourcefulness among Generation X, distinguishing them from their predecessors, who typically had one parent at home.

This early independence significantly influenced Gen X's attitude toward work and life. Having learned to rely on themselves from a young age, they developed a self-reliant mindset, often valuing practicality and resilience.

This generation is known for its entrepreneurial spirit, cynicism about authority, and preference for a work-life balance. Their ability to adapt and thrive in less structured environments made them well-suited for the rapidly changing technological landscape of the late 20th and early 21st centuries. In the workplace, they are often seen as adaptable, innovative, and capable of working independently, traits that stem from their latchkey kid experiences.

Compared to earlier generations, Generation X is notably more ethnically diverse, with about one-third of its members identifying as nonwhite. They are also less likely to participate in organized religion and generally hold more progressive views on social issues like same-sex marriage. Despite this social liberalism that is a defining feature of this generation, it doesn't mean everyone leans strongly toward traditional liberal politics. A 2022 Gallup poll revealed that 27 percent of Gen Xers identified as Democrats and 30 percent as Republicans. Interestingly, 44 percent of Gen Xers identified as independents, a higher proportion than in previous generations.

This generation significantly reshaped the culture as well. One of the defining features of the Gen X cultural landscape in the late 1980s and 1990s was grunge music, epitomized mostly by bands like Nirvana and Pearl Jam. This generation also significantly contributed to rap and hip-hop, with influential artists like De La Soul, Tupac Shakur, and Jay-Z. Numerous Gen X entertainers, including notable figures like Queen Latifah, Jennifer Lopez, and Will Smith, demonstrated versatility by effortlessly transitioning between music, television, and film.

Moreover, they were the pioneers in experiencing the widespread availability of cable television during their formative years. A significant cultural touchstone for this generation was MTV, the cable television network that launched in 1981 and initially dedicated itself to broadcasting music videos around the clock. The impact of MTV was so profound on this generation that the term "MTV Generation" became synonymous with Generation X, reflecting their deep connection to the music and pop culture promoted by the network.

Generation X, in particular, faced many challenges as well as they matured during a period marked by significant social and global upheavals. The AIDS epidemic emerged in the 1980s, bringing a sense of urgency to public health and the concept of "safe sex" practices. This health crisis influenced their awareness and attitudes toward sexual behavior, making them more cautious and responsible in intimate relationships. The epidemic's impact on society left a lasting imprint on Gen Xers, shaping their views on health, safety, and the importance of awareness and education.

Furthermore, the political landscape of the era profoundly influenced Generation X's perception of government and its responses to unfolding events. The frequent shifts in political power, combined with significant global changes, fostered a sense of skepticism and wariness toward governmental institutions among Gen Xers. The end of the Cold War was a defining moment for Generation X, as they witnessed the fall of the Berlin Wall in 1989 and the dissolution of the Soviet Union in 1991. These historical events signified a shift in global power dynamics and the promise of a new world order. Gen Xers experienced hope and uncertainty while navigating a rapidly changing geopolitical landscape. The collapse of longstanding political barriers and the emergence of new alliances and conflicts influenced their understanding of international relations and their place in a global society.

These experiences cultivated a unique political outlook in Generation X, often characterized by a preference for pragmatism over ideology. The disillusionment with traditional political structures led many Gen Xers to adopt a more independent and less partisan stance, seeking practical solutions rather than adhering strictly to party lines. Their formative years were marked by their leaders' desire for greater accountability and transparency, influencing their voting behaviors and political activism.

The changing political environment also prompted Gen Xers to become more engaged in social and cultural issues, advocating for reforms and pushing for progress in civil rights, environmental protection, and technological innovation. This engagement was driven by their firsthand experiences of political instability and a desire to create a more just and equitable society. As a result, Generation X developed a distinct political identity characterized by a balance of skepticism and active participation in shaping their communities and the world around them.

Generation X witnessed the birth of the personal computer and the advent of the internet. Unlike millennials and Gen Z, who grew up with these technologies seamlessly integrated into their lives, Gen X had to adapt to these innovations as they emerged. This unique position gave Gen

X a blend of digital fluency and a healthy dose of skepticism – a powerful combination for navigating the complexities of digital transformation.

The adaptability and resilience that Gen X developed during this technological shift are invaluable in today's rapidly changing digital landscape. They now possess a deep understanding of analog and digital worlds, allowing them to bridge the gap between generations and technologies. This generation's experience with evolving technologies also gave them insight into foreseeing potential pitfalls and opportunities in digital innovation, making them critical players in guiding sustainable and responsible technological advancements.

Furthermore, the practical mindset often associated with Gen X enabled them to approach digital transformation with a focus on real-world applications and outcomes.

Besides, This generation's unique experiences in the fast-changing world fostered a unique set of values, including a strong emphasis on work-life balance. Unlike previous generations, who often prioritized work above all else, Gen X saw the value of balancing professional responsibilities with personal life. This push for work-life balance emerged from their desire to avoid the burnout they witnessed in their parents and to ensure they had time for family, hobbies, and self-care. As a result, flexible working hours, telecommuting, and emphasis on output rather than hours spent in the office became widely accepted and practiced, significantly altering workplace norms.

In addition to advocating for work-life balance, Gen X also contributed to the rise of the entrepreneurial spirit within the workplace. Many members of this generation have shown a strong preference for autonomy and innovation, often driven by the economic volatility they experienced during their formative years. This has translated into a workplace culture that values entrepreneurial thinking, even within traditional corporate structures. Gen Xers are known for their ability to identify opportunities, take calculated risks, and adapt to changing circumstances, making them natural leaders in fostering innovation. This spirit has led to the creation of numerous startups and small businesses and the adoption of more entrepreneurial approaches within larger organizations, promoting a culture of agility and persistent improvement.

As employers have focused heavily on cultivating millennial talent in recent years, the valuable contributions of Generation X have often been overlooked. In the following chapter, we delve deeper into how Millennials have navigated and adapted to a world largely shaped by the previous generations, particularly Generation X.

— Chapter 3 —
MILLENNIALS - AVOCADO TOAST AND CRIPPLING DEBT

Initially called Generation Y, the Millennial Generation refers to individuals born between 1981 and 1996. The term "Millennial" gained popularity because this generation was born around the turn of the millennium. Representing the largest age cohort in modern history, Millennials have significantly impacted contemporary culture and society.

Born into a rapidly advancing technological world, Millennials came of age at the dawn of a new millennium. They were old enough to understand the significance of events like 9/11, which shaped their worldview. This generation has grown up alongside significant technological advancements, making them adept with digital tools and platforms.

Millennials are considered more progressive, creative, and forward-thinking than previous generations. According to the Pew Research Center, many in this generation prioritize intrinsic and moral values over materialistic ones. This value shift has influenced various aspects of society, from workplace expectations to consumer behavior and social activism.

As the youngest Millennials have reached adulthood, how do they compare to previous generations at the same age? Generally, they are better educated, which is closely linked to their employment prospects and financial stability. However, a notable economic disparity exists between those with a college education and those without. Millennials have also contributed to increased racial and ethnic diversity in American society. Like Generation X women, Millennial women are more likely to participate in the workforce than earlier generations.

Millennials between 22 and 37 years old in 2018 tend to delay or avoid marriage and are slower to establish their own households compared to their predecessors. They are also more likely to live with their parents for extended periods.

Millennials are now the second-largest generation in the U.S. electorate, following the Baby Boomers. Their significant presence continues to influence the country's politics, especially given their tendency to lean Democratic compared to older generations.

Millennials have faced various challenges as adults that have significantly shaped their economic and social experiences in the modern world. One of the most impactful events was entering the job market during the Great Recession, which began in 2007 and lasted until 2009. This economic downturn resulted in high unemployment rates, reduced job opportunities, and lower starting salaries for many Millennials. The timing of the recession coincided with the early career stages for many in this generation, leading to long-term effects on their career trajectories, income potential, and financial stability. The lack of opportunities forced many Millennials to take jobs outside their fields of study, accept lower wages, or remain underemployed, which has had lasting repercussions on their overall economic prospects.

In addition to the economic challenges posed by the Great Recession, Millennials have also had to contend with the skyrocketing costs of higher education. Over the past few decades, the cost of college tuition has increased dramatically, leading to higher levels of student loan debt. This financial burden has made it difficult for many of them to achieve traditional milestones such as buying a home, starting a family, or saving for retirement, which their predecessors were able to do easily. The pressure of student loan repayments has forced many to delay or forgo these milestones, impacting their overall financial health and stability.

Despite individual earnings for young workers staying relatively stagnant over the past five decades, there is a significant earnings disparity between Millennials with a college degree and those without. This educational divide is also evident in household income trends, which vary greatly depending on educational attainment. When it comes to household wealth, Millennials have generally accumulated slightly less compared to previous generations at the same stage in life.

More recently, Millennials have been grappling with a cost of living crisis that has further strained their financial resources. Housing prices, healthcare costs, and everyday expenses have risen sharply worldwide, often outpacing wage growth. This has made it increasingly difficult for this generation to afford basic necessities, let alone save for the future. The economic strain is compounded by the fact that many Millennials also support aging parents or start their own families, adding additional financial pressures. In spite of these challenges, Millennials have shown resilience and adaptability, often turning to gig economy jobs, side hustles, and innovative ways to manage their finances. However, the combination of entering the workforce during an economic downturn, bearing the burden of substantial student debt, and facing a high cost of living continues to pose significant hurdles for this generation.

The advent of social media fundamentally changed how Millennials communicate, form relationships, and express themselves, creating a distinct cultural reality when compared to previous generations. Social media platforms such as Facebook, Twitter, Instagram, and Snapchat have revolutionized communication by enabling instant, real-time interaction regardless of geographical location. Millennials, being the first generation to adopt these platforms, have embraced the new reality of using social media to stay connected with friends and family, share their experiences, and engage with a global audience. This constant connectivity has fostered a sense of immediacy and intimacy in their interactions, differing from the more delayed and formal communication methods favored by older generations.

The way this generation builds intimate relationships has also completely changed due to social media. Platforms like Tinder, Bumble, and OkCupid have popularized online dating, making meeting potential partners outside traditional social circles and communities easier. Social media also allows for the cultivation of broader, more diverse networks, as Millennials can effortlessly connect with people who share similar interests, hobbies, or professional goals. This has led to a more expansive and inclusive approach to personal and professional relationships. However, it has also introduced challenges, such as managing the pressures of presenting a curated online persona and dealing with issues like cyberbullying and the erosion of privacy.

This generation's self-expression has also been significantly influenced by social media, providing Millennials with various platforms to showcase their identities, talents, and opinions. Sites like Instagram and YouTube have become arenas for creative expression, where individuals can share everything from art and music to daily vlogs and personal stories. This democratization of content creation has empowered Millennials to shape their own narratives and influence cultural trends. Moreover, social media has given rise to new forms of activism and social movements, allowing Millennials to mobilize quickly and advocate for causes they care about. Compared to previous generations, Millennials' cultural reality is more dynamic, participatory, and visually oriented, driven by the continuous evolution of digital technologies and the pervasive influence of social media.

Moreover, when it comes to starting a family, millennials are generally starting families later than previous generations. According to Pew Research, only 46% of Millennials aged 25 to 37 are married, compared to a striking 83% of the Silent Generation at the same age in 1968. The percentage of married 25- to 37-year-olds has consistently decreased with each subsequent generation: 67% for early Baby Boomers and 57% for Generation X. This trend aligns with a broader societal shift toward marrying later in life. In 1968, the average American woman married at 21 and the average man at 23. Today, those ages have increased to 28 for women and 30 for men.

However, the trend isn't solely about delaying marriage. The proportion of adults who have never married is rising with each new generation. If current trends persist, approximately one in four of today's young adults will remain unmarried by their mid-40s to early 50s, marking a record-high rate. This shift highlights significant changes in societal norms and individual priorities regarding marriage and family life.

Millennial spending habits reflect a shift in values and priorities that distinguish them from previous generations. One notable example often cited in discussions about Millennial spending is their preference for "avocado toast" – a symbol of their inclination toward spending on premium food and dining experiences. This culinary preference represents a broader trend among Millennials to prioritize quality, artisanal products, and unique dining experiences over traditional consumer goods. They are willing to pay more for organic, locally sourced, and ethically produced foods, reflecting their broader values around health, sustainability, and social responsibility.

Another significant aspect of Millennial spending is their strong preference for the experience economy. Rather than accumulating material possessions, Millennials tend to spend their money on experiences such as travel, concerts, festivals, and dining out. This generation values memorable, Instagram-worthy moments and the social capital gained from sharing these experiences with their networks. The focus on experiences over things is driven by a desire for personal growth, adventure, and the enjoyment of life's fleeting moments. This shift has influenced various industries, leading to businesses catering to experiential consumption, such as travel agencies, event planning services, and entertainment venues.

However, the myth that this generation is not saving at all is still a myth, as research shows that millennials are actually saving more than previous generations did when they were in that age bracket. Millennials' approach to money and savings differs significantly from previous generations. Having come of age during the Great Recession, many Millennials are more cautious and financially conservative.

Despite these challenges, Millennials tend to invest in experiences and values that enhance their quality of life. They are more likely to use financial technology and apps to manage their money, preferring digital budgeting, investing, and banking solutions. This generation's perception of money is shaped by a blend of cautiousness, driven by economic instability, and a desire to spend on meaningful, value-driven experiences.

Contrary to popular belief, Millennials excel at saving. Research by RBA indicates that a Millennial born in the 1990s typically saves about 13% of their income, surpassing the savings rate of individuals born in the early 1970s at the same age. Additionally, Millennials are more likely to consistently report regular saving habits.

Mental illness or disorders are often more stigmatized among older generations like Generation X, where the topic is frequently seen as taboo and surrounded by various misconceptions. In contrast, there has been a significant shift in attitudes with Generation Y, who have championed increased awareness and acceptance of mental health issues. This change in perspective has been driven, in part, by the higher prevalence of mental health challenges faced by Millennials as they navigated economic downturns, skyrocketing student debt, and the pressures of modern life.

As the economy deteriorated and financial pressures mounted, Millennials experienced heightened levels of anxiety, depression, and stress. This generation's openness to discussing mental health has played a crucial role in breaking down the stigmas associated with these conditions. By advocating for mental health awareness, Millennials have helped shift public perception, encouraging more people to seek help and support.

The momentum generated by Millennials in promoting mental health awareness has had far-reaching effects. Their willingness to speak openly about their struggles has fostered a more accepting and supportive environment for those dealing with mental health issues. This generational shift has also influenced workplaces, educational institutions, and healthcare systems to prioritize mental health initiatives and provide better resources for those in need. As a result, the conversation around mental health has become more normalized, paving the way for future generations to continue addressing these critical issues without fear of stigma or judgment.

A significant development in recent years is the advent of online therapy, which has revolutionized access to mental health support. This approach has been particularly beneficial for Millennials, who are adept with digital technologies. Online therapy offers a convenient and accessible way for people to receive mental health care, removing barriers such as geographic limitations and time constraints.

Contrary to the common stereotypes of Millennials as self-centered, narcissistic, and politically apathetic, this generation holds more progressive views than older generations on various issues, ranging from LGBTQ+ rights to capitalism. Furthermore, many Millennials have actively participated in social movements to advocate for these beliefs. For the analysis, here are four major Millennial-led movements: the Dreamers, the 2011 Occupy Wall Street (OWS) uprising, the campus movement against sexual assault, and Black Lives Matter (BLM).

Karl Mannheim's seminal 1927 essay, "The Problem of Generations," helps shed light on how U.S. Millennials represent a distinct political generation characterized by unique experiences and perspectives that set them apart from previous generations of young activists. Known commonly as "digital natives," Millennials have been profoundly influenced by the Internet and new technologies throughout their lives, leading to an unprecedented scale and effectiveness in their use of network-based communication, particularly social media.

The trends of precarious and polarized employment began before the Great Recession but were intensified by it, further fueling Millennial activism, especially among the college-educated. These economic hardships have shaped their worldviews and galvanized their involvement in social and political movements, marking them as a generation driven by a desire for systemic change and greater social justice.

Millennials in the U.S. are more racially and ethnically diverse than any previous generation, having come of age in what was often touted as a post-racial society. However, they continue to face enduring racism. Despite assertions that gender inequality has been largely resolved, Millennials frequently encounter significant disparities in how women and men are treated, alongside systematic discrimination against sexual minorities. Additionally, this generation is deeply affected by escalating class inequality and the overwhelming political influence wielded by corporations and wealthy individuals.

The Millennial perspective merges the identity politics of the New Left from the 1960s with the traditional critiques of class inequality and capitalism championed by the Old Left in the 1930s. This synthesis has spurred thousands of Millennials to become politically active, especially in the wake of the 2008 financial crisis. Their engagement in social movements—such as the Dreamers, Occupy Wall Street, the campaign against campus sexual assault, and Black Lives Matter—demonstrates their commitment to addressing both identity-based and economic injustices.

Collectively, these movements that emerged after 2008 indicate the rise of a new wave of left-wing protests. They have already influenced U.S. political culture and could potentially lead to lasting social change. These movements have arisen amidst a deeply polarized political environment, juxtaposed by various right-wing populist movements supported by dissatisfied older white demographics. The outcome of this clash between these starkly different alternatives remains uncertain, but the momentum appears to favor the younger generation over time.

— Chapter 4 —
GEN Z - DIGITAL NATIVES AND MEME LORDS

Generation Z, typically defined as those born after 1996, is the first generation to grow up in a world dominated by digital technology. This cohort has been immersed in the internet, smartphones, and social media from a young age, profoundly shaping their experiences and worldview. Unlike previous generations, Gen Z has never known a time without instant access to information, online connectivity, and digital communication, making them uniquely adapted to the fast-changing, technology-driven environment of the 21st century.

Exposure to such technology from birth has equipped Gen Z with the ability to process vast amounts of information quickly. They are adept at navigating multiple screens simultaneously and can effortlessly switch between tasks such as homework, social media, music, videos, and live conversations. This multitasking capability allows them to absorb and analyze information more efficiently than previous generations, enabling them to grow up quickly in an increasingly complex world. As a result, they are often characterized by their ability to learn and adapt rapidly, essential skills in today's ever-evolving digital landscape.

Growing up during a period of significant innovation, social transformation, and more favorable economic conditions, Generation Z tends to be more optimistic about the future. Unlike Millennials, who delayed traditional milestones such as marriage, purchasing a car, or buying a house by 5-8 years, Gen Z is eager to embark on their adult lives and gain independence. They are keen to move out and establish their own paths much earlier.

This generation is characterized by their early entrepreneurial spirit, setting their sights on building their futures with purpose and ambition. They value meaningful challenges over constant praise, seeking fulfillment through impactful work and personal growth. While they share many social, cultural, and political views with Millennials, Gen Z is pushing these transformations even further. They are more proactive in addressing issues like climate change, social justice, and equality, and their innovative use of technology amplifies their influence.

Gen Z's readiness to embrace change and forward-thinking mindset drive significant cultural and societal shifts. They are not only inheriting the progress made by Millennials but are also expanding it, leveraging their unique skillsets and perspectives to create a more inclusive, equitable, and dynamic society. Their confidence and proactive approach to handling life's challenges position them as key agents of change in the coming decades.

Generation Z, often referred to as true digital natives, stands apart from Millennials in their relationship with technology. While Millennials experienced the advent and evolution of the internet, social media, and smartphones, Gen Z has grown up in an era of ubiquitous technology. This generation has never known a world without the internet, making them inherently adept at integrating technology into every facet of their lives.

Gen Z's comfort with rapid technological advancements is unparalleled. They naturally adapt to new platforms and innovations, favoring visual communication methods on apps like TikTok and Instagram. These platforms cater to their preference for quick, engaging content, allowing them to express themselves creatively and connect with others instantaneously. Unlike previous generations, Gen Z uses technology not just as a tool but as an extension of their identity, seamlessly merging their online and offline lives.

This generation's fluency in digital media extends beyond social interaction. They utilize technology for a wide range of activities, from education and work to entertainment and self-expression. Video content, memes, and digital storytelling are integral to their communication style, reflecting their desire for immediacy and visual engagement. As a result, Gen Z has developed a unique cultural identity heavily influenced by their digital experiences, setting them apart as digital natives.

Generation Z exhibits a distinct attitude toward education and career, emphasizing the importance of higher education and practical skills. According to Pew Research, this generation has the highest college enrollment rate, with 59% of Gen Z members pursuing higher education. Additionally, a significant number of them live with college-educated parents, contributing to their academic aspirations and achievements.

This emphasis on education is reflected in their impressive statistics. Gen Z boasts the lowest high school dropout rate, at just 6%, compared to 12% for Millennials in 2002. However, they are also the least employed, with only 58% holding jobs compared to 72% of Millennials. About one-third of Gen Z lives with a single parent (31%), which is slightly higher than the 27% of Millennials. Despite these challenges, high school completion rates have shown modest gains for this generation, with 80% of Gen Z finishing high school compared to 78% of Millennials.

The most notable improvements are seen among Hispanic and Black youth. Hispanic high school completion rates jumped from 60% to 78%, and Black youth increased from 71% to 77%, narrowing the gap with their white peers at 81%. Asian students continue to lead with a 90% completion rate. Similar trends are observed in college enrollment, where there have been modest gains for whites (61%) and Asians (80%). Hispanic youth saw significant improvement, with enrollment rates rising from 34% to 55%, while Black youth increased from 47% to 54%. These statistics underscore Gen Z's commitment to education and their pursuit of opportunities for higher learning and career advancement.

As Millennials are known for seeking purpose and meaning in their careers, placing a high value on work-life balance, and gravitating toward companies with strong ethical standards and social responsibility commitments. Gen Z on the other hand, has a different approach. They prioritize flexibility and entrepreneurial opportunities over traditional career paths. Gen Z is less inclined to commit to a single employer and more interested in gig economy jobs, freelance work, and entrepreneurial ventures. This generation values work environments that allow for personal growth and adaptability, often favoring remote work options and non-traditional career structures. They seek roles that offer the freedom to explore various interests and the ability to balance work with personal life more fluidly.

Younger Americans, specifically Millennials and Generation Z adults, are notably more engaged with climate change, according to a new Pew Research Center survey. Compared to older generations, Gen Z and Millennials are more vocal about the necessity for climate action. Social media users within these groups encounter more climate change content online, and they are more actively involved in the cause through volunteering, attending rallies, and participating in protests. Their heightened awareness and proactive stance on climate issues highlight a generational shift toward greater environmental activism.

This generation believes in sustainability and environmental responsibility, often participating in climate strikes, supporting green policies, and holding corporations and governments accountable for their wrong policies that are destroying Earth. Their activism is driven by a sense of urgency and a desire to ensure a livable planet for future generations.

Moreover, School shootings and escalating political polarization in the U.S. have profoundly shaped Generation Z's political culture and identity, impacting their views and activism in significant ways.

Growing up amid frequent reports of school shootings has instilled a strong sense of urgency and advocacy for gun control within Gen Z. Many members of this generation have directly experienced lockdown drills or have known someone affected by such violence, leading them to prioritize safety and legislation aimed at preventing gun violence. The trauma and fear associated with these events have galvanized Gen Z into action, with many young activists emerging as vocal leaders in the push for stricter gun control measures. Movements like March for Our Lives, spearheaded by survivors of the Parkland shooting, exemplify how Gen Z is channeling their experiences into powerful calls for change.

Furthermore, the heightened political polarization in recent years has further influenced Gen Z's political engagement. Exposed to divisive rhetoric and partisan conflicts, this generation has become keenly aware of the importance of political participation and advocacy.

Nevertheless, the key to Generation Z's political influence lies in their ability to mobilize and support one another. Despite nearly half of voters aged 18-29 not being directly contacted by political campaigns in 2020, as reported by the Tufts Research Center, Gen Z still achieved a high turnout in that election. This success is largely attributed to their adept use of social media to connect, share information, and rally around issues they care about. They engage with community groups and leverage digital platforms to advocate for their causes, effectively organizing and motivating each other without traditional campaign outreach. According to Kawashima-Ginsberg, this self-reliant and interconnected approach demonstrates Gen Z's unique capability to drive political participation and influence through grassroots mobilization and peer support.

Generation Z's engagement with social media represents a notable shift from previous generations, fundamentally altering how they interact socially and culturally. Unlike Millennials and older cohorts, Gen Z has been raised in a digital era dominated by platforms such as Instagram, TikTok, and Twitter, which are integral to their everyday experiences. A prominent feature of this digital landscape is the emergence of influencer culture, where individuals attain prominence and sway through their online activities. Gen Z frequently turns to these influencers not only for fashion trends and lifestyle tips but also for political perspectives, influencing their consumer behaviors and societal standards.

Studies indicate that about 65% of teenage girls in the United States dedicate around two hours and forty minutes each day to TikTok. This time surpasses that spent on other social media platforms, underscoring TikTok's distinctive allure for this age group. TikTok's captivating content and its knack for delivering a continuous flow of fresh and pertinent videos likely contribute to the extended durations users spend on the platform.

While TikTok offers entertainment and a platform for creative expression among teenage girls, it is crucial to acknowledge the potential consequences of excessive social media consumption on mental health and overall wellness.

In the contemporary digital age, where content is ubiquitous and constantly evolving, memes have emerged as a distinctive cultural phenomenon, especially resonating with Generation Z, often dubbed the "meme lords." Memes, which are humorous images, videos, or text shared rapidly across social media platforms, encapsulate complex ideas and emotions succinctly and entertainingly. This form of communication aligns perfectly with the fast-paced, visually oriented preferences of Gen Z and Millennials.

Nonetheless, the influence of meme culture extends beyond entertainment; it also shapes political and social discourse. For Gen Z, memes are not just about jokes but also about making statements on current events, societal issues, and personal beliefs. This generation uses memes to raise awareness, mobilize activism, and critique the status quo, demonstrating the profound impact of this seemingly simple medium. As a result, memes have become a crucial element in how Gen Z navigates and interprets the world, reflecting their unique blend of creativity, tech-savviness, and social consciousness.

Generation Z stands out for its acute awareness of mental health issues and understanding the multifaceted challenges faced in today's world. This generation is actively destigmatizing mental health issues by leveraging social media to share personal stories, promote awareness campaigns, and support peers facing similar challenges. Influencers and online communities play a crucial role in normalizing mental health conversations, using hashtags like #MentalHealthAwareness and #EndTheStigma to foster open discussions. Their proactive approach is reshaping the dialogue around mental well-being as they advocate for education, policy changes, and accessible resources, making significant strides in addressing the mental health crisis and supporting each other.

This generation is also notably the most racially and ethnically diverse in American history, with nearly half of its members being non-white (48%). A significant portion of Gen Z, about 25%, identifies as Hispanic, a marked increase from the 18% of Millennials at the same age in 2002.

Importantly, according to demographic data shared by Pew Research, the majority of Hispanic Gen Z individuals were born in the United States, with only 12% being immigrants, compared to 24% among Millennials. Although the overall percentage of foreign-born youth has remained relatively stable from Millennials to Gen Z (8% and 7%, respectively), there is a notable increase in the number of Gen Z individuals with at least one immigrant parent—22% compared to 15% for Millennials. This shift highlights the growing influence of second-generation immigrants on the demographic composition of Gen Z.

Even with lower immigration flows in recent years, the racial and ethnic diversity of Gen Z is projected to continue expanding. As new immigrants integrate into the population, the diversity within this generation is expected to rise further. Current projections indicate that Gen Z will become majority non-white by 2026, underscoring the significant and ongoing impact of immigration and demographic changes on the composition of America's youngest generation. This diverse background fosters a broad, inclusive perspective among Gen Z, further influencing their views on social issues and shaping a more interconnected, multicultural society.

— Chapter 5 —
GEN ALPHA - THE FUTURE IS NOW

Generation Alpha, the cohort succeeding Generation Z, encompasses individuals born from 2013 onward, with their parents predominantly being Millennials (born between 1981 and 1996), as per Pew Research Center. The term "Generation Alpha" was coined by demographer Mark McCrindle in 2005, who founded the Australian consultancy firm McCrindle. McCrindle chose this name to signify a fresh start, stating, "In keeping with the scientific tradition of using the Greek alphabet instead of the Latin, and having already worked through Generations X, Y, and Z, we decided on Generation Alpha—not a return to the old, but the beginning of something new." This terminology reflects the expectation that Generation Alpha will experience and influence a world markedly different from their predecessors.

Generation Alpha is anticipated to be the most technologically adept and digitally empowered generation to date. Born into a world filled with smartphones, AI, and the Internet of Things, they will interact with an array of digital devices from a young age, with their screen time expected to surpass that of any previous generation. This unprecedented level of engagement with technology will shape their learning, communication, and entertainment experiences in ways that are yet to be fully understood. As they navigate a world where digital interaction is the norm, they will develop skills and behaviors uniquely suited to a highly connected environment.

This extensive exposure to technology can be viewed as a grand social experiment, the outcomes of which remain uncertain for now. While Generation Alpha's digital proficiency may bring numerous advantages, such as enhanced problem-solving abilities and global connectivity, there are also potential risks, including impacts on attention spans, social skills, and mental health. Researchers and educators are closely monitoring this generation to understand the long-term effects of their digital immersion. They recognize that how this generation engages with technology will profoundly influence their development and the future societal landscape.

The age at which we encounter transformative events greatly influences how deeply they affect us, and COVID-19 is anticipated to be a defining moment for Generation Alpha. A significant majority of adults (84%) believe that COVID-19 will profoundly impact today's children. While the full extent of this influence will unfold over time, many children, the oldest of whom turned 11 in 2020, will retain memories of this global crisis. They observed their parents working from makeshift home offices while they attended virtual classrooms. Although they might not fully understand the reasons behind social distancing, they know it's necessary. The reality of being unable to visit parks or see grandparents for extended periods is something they won't forget. When surveyed about the potential long-term impacts of COVID-19 on this generation, responses highlighted the integration of technology into daily life, evolving expectations around work environments, and the normalization of online education.

The COVID-19 pandemic has undoubtedly accelerated technology integration into education, highlighting its potential while emphasizing the irreplaceable value of face-to-face and tactile learning. The education sector quickly adapted to social distancing measures, which brought about a host of challenges. Despite these hurdles, 71% of parents who kept their children at home reported a predominantly positive experience, and 82% of adults believe that online education will become more prevalent in the future.

However, the absence of traditional schooling during lockdowns was deeply felt, not only by overwhelmed parents trying to balance their work with supervising their children's education but also by communities that rely on schools for social interaction. Schools serve as vital community hubs, fostering a sense of belonging and interaction that goes beyond academic learning.

For Generation Alpha, already growing up in a tech-driven world, the pandemic has further entrenched digital interactions in their daily lives. This generation has become accustomed to using platforms like Zoom and participating in virtual environments due to COVID-19. As a result, we might see them innovating and engaging with technology in increasingly creative and sophisticated ways while also recognizing the importance of in-person experiences and physical interactions in their holistic development.

Generation Alpha will come of age in a world deeply influenced by Artificial Intelligence, fundamentally altering their experiences and daily lives. Just as previous generations witnessed the transformative impact of technologies like the Internet, Gen Alpha will be the first to navigate a future where AI is deeply integrated into every facet of life. The influence of AI will be pervasive, molding their future in ways that are currently beyond our full comprehension.

Generation Alpha will grow up in a world teeming with virtual assistants, smart systems, and AI-powered appliances, all designed to simplify their lives and enhance efficiency. From virtual assistants like Alexa and Google Home managing daily tasks to smart refrigerators that automatically order groceries when supplies run low, AI will seamlessly integrate into their everyday routines. In healthcare, AI will enable personalized medicine, predicting health issues before they arise and offering tailored treatments, thereby improving overall wellness and safety.

Additionally, advanced security systems utilizing facial recognition and machine learning will provide enhanced protection in homes and public spaces. This generation will interact with a digital future where the line between the virtual and the real is becoming thin, thanks to sophisticated gadgets and software driven by complex interaction algorithms, making technology a natural and ubiquitous part of their lives.

Moreover, AI is set to revolutionize the way this new generation communicates. Traditionally, a shared language has been essential for interaction, but this necessity is becoming a thing of the past with the advent of devices like the Apple Vision Pro. Picture this: you encounter someone from a different country, and instead of grappling with language barriers, you simply use your device. The Apple Vision Pro, or a similar device, instantly translates your speech, enabling real-time conversation in any language. This technological leap will make cross-border communication seamless and effortless, breaking down language barriers and fostering greater global connectivity. This innovation enhances personal interactions and has profound implications for international business, travel, and cultural exchange, making the world more interconnected than ever before.

For Generation Alpha, the climate crisis is a pivotal issue that will shape their entire future. They are likely to witness the world transition into the 2100s, an era that could either be characterized by severe climate catastrophes or averted through decisive actions taken today. The urgency is undeniable, as the choices made in the 2020s will determine the environmental landscape they inherit.

This generation is also the first to grow up in a world where technology is omnipresent from birth. They are the infants soothed by an iPad, lulled to sleep by white noise from an iPhone, and engaged by digital content from an early age. This early and constant interaction with technology will profoundly influence their development, learning, and socialization. As they grow older, their familiarity with digital tools and platforms will shape their approach to problem-solving, communication, and activism. Generation Alpha is uniquely positioned to leverage technology in addressing global challenges, including climate change, making its role in shaping the future both critical and transformative.

The way Generation Alpha is being raised will significantly influence workplace cultures in the future as global technological standards continue to evolve and integrate. Born into a world where digital connectivity blurs geographical and cultural boundaries, Gen Alpha will carry this global perspective into their professional lives. As a result, they will foster even more inclusive and diverse workplace environments where cross-continental and cross-cultural collaborations become commonplace. This shift will encourage a more interconnected and cooperative approach to work, breaking down barriers and enriching the global workforce.

Generation Alpha is poised to redefine social norms, work culture, and global connectivity in ways we can't yet fully envision. Growing up with advanced technology, they will likely challenge traditional social conventions, advocating for more inclusive, flexible, and digital-centric lifestyles.

— Part II —
Why Can't We All Just Get Along?

— Chapter 6 —
"OK Boomer" vs. "Kids These Days"

For a considerable time, the conversation between baby boomers and millennials has centered on recurring criticisms. Baby boomers, born between 1946 and 1965, frequently accuse millennials of entitlement, suggesting they expect accolades for minimal effort. Conversely, millennials, born between 1980 and 1996, argue that boomers are out of touch with current realities. Millennials feel blamed for the decline of traditional industries, such as cereal, because they prioritize saving money and make different spending choices, like buying avocados. They also contend that boomers have compromised the future by hoarding wealth and dismantling essential social programs. In turn, millennials are often portrayed as complainers who focus on student debt rather than working hard and finding employment.

Teens, particularly those of Generation Z (born between 1996 and 2015), have faced even harsher criticisms. They are often depicted as phone-obsessed, "intolerant" of older generations, and living in a "different world" due to the internet.

Amid this endless bickering, it's no surprise that the most polarizing meme of the year is the two-word retort, "OK, boomer." This catchphrase, which gained widespread popularity this fall, is a way for millennials and Gen Z to succinctly summarize and dismiss the ongoing generational debate.

The origin of this catchphrase, "OK Boomer," first appeared as early as 2015 on 4chan, where anonymous users employed it as an insult directed at older generations whom they perceived as being out of touch. Nevertheless, In early November 2019, a TikTok video featured a grey-haired man, likely a Baby Boomer (born 1946-1964), stating that "millennials and

Generation Z have Peter Pan syndrome," implying they refuse to grow up. On the other side of the split-screen, a Gen Zer (born 1995-2015) silently holds up a notepad that says, "OK, Boomer." The phrase quickly went viral, spawning numerous variations of the video. By mid-November, the hashtag #OKBoomer had been used over 732 million times, and more than 2,000 hoodies with the slogan "OK Boomer, have a terrible day" had been sold for $34.99 each.

In these videos, teens often highlight typical generational disagreements. However, their reactions are often politically charged, addressing criticisms from adults about their gender expression, financial decisions, job-hunting strategies, or leisure activities. The underlying frustration stems from the perceived irony that while boomers critique the younger generations' choices, it is actually the boomers' decisions that have shaped the challenging socioeconomic landscape that Millennials and Gen Z now navigate.

For Millennials and Gen Z, the "OK Boomer" meme encapsulates the frustration and disconnection they feel with the older generation's lack of understanding about the real-life challenges they will inherit. These two words resonate deeply, especially after years of being blamed for the decline of various industries, from restaurant chains to department stores to traditional relationships. Young people see this criticism as misplaced; they argue that many of their struggles—student loan debt, economic instability, and the looming threat of climate change—stem from the shortsighted decisions made by earlier generations. This simple phrase has become a powerful symbol of their exasperation and a succinct way to push back against the narrative that they are responsible for problems they did not create.

As the "OK Boomer" meme gained mainstream traction, its deeper socioeconomic implications were largely overlooked. The meme initially served as a pointed critique of older generations and their impact on current economic and social challenges. However, its widespread popularity surged after an October New York Times article highlighted teens who had turned the meme into merchandise and fashion statements. This commercialization saw a rush to sell "OK Boomer" products, with individuals and companies seeking to trademark the phrase and brands using it in their marketing campaigns. This commodification ironically missed the meme's underlying criticism of capitalism, prompting further eye-rolling from the younger generations who saw the irony in a critique of capitalism being used for profit.

From a social science perspective, stereotypes about each generation significantly shape people's perceptions and interactions, often reinforcing existing social divides and influencing intergenerational dynamics. These broad generalizations—like labeling Millennials as "lazy" and Boomers as "grumpy"—create a framework through which individuals interpret the behaviors and attitudes of people from different age groups.

For instance, the stereotype of Millennials as entitled and averse to hard work can lead to biases in the workplace, where older generations might view their younger colleagues with skepticism, questioning their commitment and work ethic. This can result in strained professional relationships, with Millennials feeling misunderstood and undervalued, perpetuating a cycle of mistrust and miscommunication. Conversely, the characterization of Boomers as resistant to change and out of touch can lead younger generations to dismiss their experiences and perspectives, potentially overlooking valuable insights and wisdom that come with age and experience.

These stereotypes are more than just harmless labels; they have real consequences on interactions between different age groups. They can shape hiring decisions, workplace interactions, and even family dynamics, often fostering a lack of empathy and understanding across generations. Furthermore, these stereotypes are commonly reinforced by media portrayals and societal narratives, which can intensify and perpetuate intergenerational conflicts.

To grasp why different generations exhibit distinct behaviors and motivations, social science offers a framework for examining these generational differences and the underlying reasons for their unique patterns of conduct.

The social science perspective on intergenerational criticism involves examining several psychological mechanisms that drive these attitudes. Two key concepts are in-group bias and the fundamental attribution error.

In-group Bias refers to the tendency to favor one's own group over others. This psychological phenomenon, studied extensively by social psychologists like Henri Tajfel and John Turner, suggests that individuals view their own generation (or "in-group") more favorably compared to others. This bias can lead to negative stereotypes about other generations, as people tend to overlook the positive attributes of out-group members and emphasize their flaws. This favoritism can distort perceptions, making generational differences appear more pronounced and contributing to criticisms that may not fully acknowledge the complexities of other generations' experiences.

The concept known as the fundamental attribution error, as elucidated by social psychologists, describes how people tend to explain others' behavior by attributing it to internal traits or dispositions rather than considering external situational factors. In the context of intergenerational criticism, this phenomenon suggests that individuals may attribute negative behaviors or characteristics of other generations to inherent traits (like laziness or incompetence), overlooking broader social, economic, or cultural influences that shape behavior, which explains the behavior of boomers toward the younger generations and vice versa.

Social psychologists such as Harold Kelley and Bernard Weiner have also studied how people's perceptions of others' actions influence how they see each other. They've shown that it's crucial to think about the situations people are in when we judge their behavior, especially when comparing different groups or generations. This highlights that assuming someone's actions are only because of their personal traits can cause misunderstandings and biases in how different generations interact with each other.

People should recall how, just a few years ago, every headline focused on what was supposedly wrong with millennials, and now the spotlight has shifted to Gen Z. Remember when the media squarely blamed Boomers for the housing crisis? The truth is that the media thrives on clickbait headlines, which serve a purpose but often lead to generalized resentment and misunderstandings among generations. These headlines fail to encourage a deeper examination of broader factors or the political, economic, and social contexts that shaped each generation under those unique circumstances.

In today's interconnected world, where information inundates us constantly, escaping the adverse effects of social media can be challenging, and it eventually exacerbates generational differences. Clickbait headlines are designed to capture attention quickly, often through sensationalism, exaggeration, or emotionally charged language. These headlines frequently exploit generational stereotypes by highlighting conflict or differences between age groups, such as portraying Baby Boomers as out of touch or Millennials and Gen Z as overly sensitive or lethargic. This not only reinforces negative stereotypes but also deepens misunderstandings and animosities between generations. When users click on these provocative headlines, they are often led to content that oversimplifies complex issues, further entrenching their preconceptions and biases.

Moreover, the algorithmic nature of social media platforms means that clickbait headlines are more likely to be promoted and shared, especially if they elicit strong reactions. This creates echo chambers where users are repeatedly exposed to content that confirms their existing beliefs and stereotypes about other generations. As a result, intergenerational conflicts are magnified, and the nuanced understanding necessary for meaningful dialogue and mutual respect is undermined. This cycle of sensationalism and stereotype reinforcement contributes to a fragmented society where generational divisions are perpetuated and amplified.

As a result, these generational differences that were caused by various things, including the media's portrayal of them and people's biases against each other, manifest in tangible ways across various facets of life. In workplaces, differences in work styles, communication preferences, and attitudes toward authority often lead to tensions among different age groups. According to recent surveys in the US, such as those conducted by Pew Research Center and Gallup, intergenerational conflicts are increasingly recognized as a significant issue impacting productivity and morale in organizations. Millennials, for instance, may be perceived as seeking rapid advancement and work-life balance, contrasting with older generations who prioritize job loyalty and hierarchical structures. These clashes have been hindering collaboration and innovation, ultimately affecting businesses and the outcomes they've been trying to achieve in the long run.

Moreover, generational divisions are starkly evident in political arenas, influencing voting patterns and policy priorities. As stated previously, the 2020 US election highlighted significant generational gaps, with younger voters leaning toward progressive policies on climate change, healthcare, and social justice, while older generations tended to support more conservative platforms. The rise of Donald Trump as a political figure in the United States serves as a stark reminder of the ideological divide between older and younger generations regarding liberal policies. Trump's presidency, particularly his unexpected electoral success in 2016 and the continued support he garnered throughout his tenure, underscored a significant backlash against the progressive agenda championed by younger generations. This phenomenon was particularly evident in Trump's appeal to older, predominantly white voters who felt disenfranchised by what they perceived as a shift toward more liberal and inclusive policies in the national discourse.

On the contrary, younger generations, including Millennials and Gen Z, have increasingly advocated for progressive policies such as environmental sustainability, social justice reforms, and expanded healthcare access. They have consistently thrown their support behind progressive candidates who are committed to addressing urgent challenges such as climate change and are vocal in their support for movements that prioritize diversity, equity, and inclusion, viewing these issues as crucial for addressing systemic inequalities and promoting a more inclusive society.

The stark generational divide highlighted by Trump's rise reflects broader societal shifts in values, priorities, and attitudes toward governance and social issues. It underscores the ongoing tension between maintaining established norms and embracing change, with each generation grappling with its own interpretation of what constitutes progress and how best to navigate an increasingly complex global landscape.

— Chapter 7 —
Tech Tantrums - From Rotary to TikTok

The journey from rotary phones to TikTok illustrates communication technology's profound and multifaceted evolution over the past century. In the early 20th century, rotary phones marked a significant leap forward in personal communication, moving away from the more cumbersome methods of telegrams and operator-assisted calls. The rotary phone required users to dial manually, emphasizing a systematic and deliberate approach to communication. This era laid the groundwork for future innovations, as communication was primarily face-to-face or through written correspondence, which fostered a slower, more personal exchange of information.

The transition to digital communication began in earnest with the advent of touch-tone phones in the 1960s, which made dialing more efficient and intuitive. However, the most transformative changes came with the rise of personal computers and the internet in the late 20th century. The introduction of email, early chat programs, and social networks such as AOL and MySpace revolutionized how people communicated, shifting from purely analog methods to digital. Older generations who had been accustomed to rotary phones and landline communications, adapting to these new technologies required overcoming a steep learning curve and adjusting to a faster-paced, more instantaneous mode of interaction.

In the 21st century, platforms like TikTok represent the latest evolution in digital communication, characterized by short-form video content and highly personalized user experiences. This new frontier of communication is emblematic of the dramatic shift towards rapid, visual, and interactive content, which resonates strongly with younger generations who have grown up with these technologies. The rapid adoption of such platforms has further widened the generational gap, as older individuals may struggle with the complexity and pace of these modern tools. Understanding this historical progression highlights the technological advancements and the deepening divide in digital fluency and communication preferences across different age groups.

A clear illustration of the generational technology gap is evident in the differences in communication styles between age groups. These disparities stem from varying societal norms, communication preferences, and expectations shaped by distinct technological eras. Older generations who grew up before the digital revolution typically favor direct, face-to-face interactions or traditional written communication methods. In contrast, younger generations, immersed in digital technology from an early age, predominantly use electronic communication platforms like emails, social media, and instant messaging instead of face-to-face communication.

The notion that older generations often struggle with new technology is a recurring theme across decades, illustrating the ever-evolving nature of tech and its impact on different age groups. In the 1980s, this stereotype emerged as children showed their parents how to set the clock on their VCRs—a task that, despite its apparent simplicity, proved quite challenging for many adults of that era. The 1990s brought about a new wave of technology, with children and teenagers guiding their parents through the intricacies of personal computers and the early days of online connectivity, including signing up for AOL. These were pioneering times, and as digital technology began to permeate everyday life, the gap between those who grew up with it and those who did not became increasingly wide.

By the 2000s, the landscape had shifted yet again with the proliferation of social media platforms and smartphones. Younger generations became instructors once more, teaching older adults how to navigate Facebook, Instagram, and the various functionalities of smartphones. This period marked a significant leap in technology, and even today, many find themselves fielding tech support calls from their parents regarding these technologies. The ongoing need for assistance reflects the persistent gap in digital fluency between generations, even as technology continues to advance rapidly.

Today, the advent of the "Internet of Things" (IoT) has significantly deepened the generational divide in technological expertise. With a growing array of everyday objects—from doorbells and household appliances to watches and automobiles—now equipped with smart technology, the landscape of personal and home tech has become increasingly intricate. This proliferation of interconnected devices has introduced complexity that can be daunting for older individuals who may struggle to keep pace with these advancements.

As technology continues to evolve at a breakneck speed, older generations often find themselves grappling with the multitude of features and functionalities embedded in these smart devices. This situation highlights a widening gap in digital fluency as younger generations, who are more adept at navigating such technologies, frequently take on the role of instructors. Each new technological breakthrough presents its own set of challenges, further emphasizing the ongoing need for intergenerational knowledge transfer. This dynamic underscores how rapidly changing tech landscapes influence daily life and communication, reinforcing the perpetual cycle of younger individuals guiding their elders through the complexities of modern innovation.

On the internet, memes and humorous anecdotes about intergenerational tech interactions have become a popular and poignant reflection of the digital divide between generations. These online phenomena vividly illustrate the challenges older generations face in keeping up with rapidly evolving technology while highlighting the often amusing gaps in digital literacy.

For instance, memes featuring grandparents bewildered by the complexities of FaceTime or struggling to navigate social media platforms capture the light-hearted yet real difficulties faced by those who did not grow up with modern digital tools. These moments—such as a grandparent's confused reaction to a video call or their humorous attempts to understand emoji usage—underscore the stark contrast between the tech-savvy younger generations and their less experienced elders. The comedic portrayal of such scenarios entertains and illuminates the broader issue of digital disparity.

Conversely, stories and memes about younger people's bemusement of outdated technology, like VHS tapes, provide a snapshot of how quickly technological norms shift. Younger generations, who may have never used a VHS tape or dial-up internet, often find these older technologies perplexing. These anecdotes—such as kids struggling to figure out how to rewind a tape or questioning the need for physical media—highlight how rapidly technology becomes obsolete and how each generation can struggle to bridge the gap between past and present tech.

Together, these shared experiences on social media and other online platforms serve as a source of humor and a commentary on the broader generational divide. This ongoing dialogue, framed through humor and shared stories, underscores the significant impact of technological advancements on intergenerational interactions and highlights the need for continued support and understanding across age groups in navigating the digital world.

Frustration is a common theme among younger generations when it comes to teaching older individuals how to use new technologies or appliances. This frustration is well-documented, as younger people often experience impatience when helping their elders navigate modern apps or devices. The struggle to effectively convey how these technologies work can be challenging, leading to moments of exasperation.

A relatable example shared online captures this sentiment: 'After just a few minutes trying to explain a basic function on my parents' iPhone or how Facebook works, I usually give up. I feel like the worst kind of ungrateful brat when I wish they would just get it.' This sense of impatience and frustration is common among younger generations, particularly millennials, who frequently encounter similar scenarios. This impatience often stems from a lack of shared experiences and a disconnect between generations, making it harder to bridge the gap in understanding.

It's crucial to recognize that while empathy is important, it's challenging to fully grasp the perspective of someone from a different era. People's personal experiences and cultural backgrounds shape how they interact with technology and perceive its complexities. For those who have grown up with rapid technological advancements, the learning curve for older generations can seem unusually steep. Understanding this disconnect requires acknowledging that people's own frustrations may be rooted in the difficulty of relating to experiences and perspectives vastly different from their own. By appreciating this generational gap, they can foster greater patience and develop more effective ways to support older individuals in adapting to the fast-paced world of modern technology.

To help bridge the generational gap in technology use, it's crucial to provide the older generation with accessible platforms and resources designed to address their concerns about new technologies while also educating them about current trends. One promising approach gaining traction online is the concept of digital clinics. These clinics offer a structured environment where older adults can receive hands-on guidance and support in learning about modern technology.

Digital clinics are specifically designed to address the challenges faced by older generations in adapting to new technologies. They often involve direct interaction with tech-savvy younger individuals who can provide personalized instruction and answer questions in real-time. This face-to-face interaction, which can be both in-person and virtual, helps to demystify complex technologies and makes learning more approachable. The idea is to create a supportive setting where older adults can comfortably ask questions, practice new skills, and build confidence in using digital tools.

This initiative addresses the immediate need for tech education and fosters intergenerational communication and understanding. By creating opportunities for younger generations to share their knowledge and expertise, digital clinics can help reduce the barriers that contribute to the digital divide. Additionally, these clinics can offer ongoing support and resources, ensuring that older individuals can keep up with technological advancements and remain connected in a rapidly evolving digital world. Ultimately, such programs are instrumental in bridging the gap in digital literacy and promoting smoother interactions between different generations.

Furthermore, Technology, when employed thoughtfully, has the potential to bridge generational gaps and foster closer connections between different age groups. Through various applications and platforms, technology can facilitate shared experiences and enhance communication, making it easier for people of different generations to interact and understand one another.

A notable method for bridging generational gaps through technology is by engaging in shared gaming experiences. Whether simple mobile games or more complex multiplayer platforms, online games create a common space for interaction across different age groups. Games such as "Words with

Friends" and "Animal Crossing" have gained popularity among families, enabling grandparents and grandchildren to join forces, collaborate, and enjoy friendly competition. These joint activities not only offer fun and entertainment but also build a sense of camaraderie and enhance mutual understanding between generations.

Another valuable tool for narrowing the generational divide is setting up family WhatsApp groups. These groups serve as a convenient platform for exchanging photos, videos, and updates, enabling ongoing communication between family members. For older adults who might find digital communication tools challenging at first, a family-specific group offers a supportive and stress-free setting where they can learn and become more at ease with new technology.

When technology is applied carefully and with consideration, it has the potential to bridge generational gaps by fostering shared experiences and enhancing communication. By leveraging these tools and offering support for their effective use, both younger and older generations can strengthen their connections and deepen their mutual understanding, leading to more meaningful and unified relationships across different age groups.

— Chapter 8 —
Work It - Cubicles, Gig Economy, and WFH Chaos

Change is the one unchanging aspect of existence in this universe. Everything around us, from communities to the environment and even one's own personal self, is in a state of continuous transformation. This persistent evolution necessitates adaptability in order to stay relevant and thrive in an ever-shifting world. In this context, the dynamics of workplace culture have undergone significant shifts over time, reflecting broader societal changes.

In the past, the members of the older generations were expected to show unwavering loyalty to a single company throughout their careers. This model emphasized long-term stability and a deep commitment to one employer, often with the promise of job security and a clear career progression. However, this traditional perspective has largely given way to a more fluid approach to employment, where frequent job changes are increasingly common and even encouraged. This shift highlights the changing nature of job satisfaction and career development, where new opportunities and diverse experiences are highly valued among the younger generations.

The transformation in workplace expectations mirrors broader generational changes and evolving attitudes toward work. As job-hopping becomes more prevalent, it signifies a move toward a more dynamic and flexible work environment. This evolution demands that both employees and employers adapt to new norms, embracing continuous learning and agile career paths.

The traditional 9-to-5 job model, which has been a fundamental part of the American workforce for more than a hundred years, is now experiencing significant disruption. This change is fueled by technological progress, shifting expectations among workers, and the evolving demands of businesses.

To understand this transformation better, we need to examine the key factors driving this shift and the new trends that are redefining the future of work.

Traditional 9-to-5 office jobs have long been a staple of the working world, particularly favored by older generations who thrived under such structures. In the past, stable economic conditions and company loyalty meant employees often went above and beyond their standard hours, sometimes working extended shifts to meet their bosses' needs. This dedication was fueled by a sense of job security and the prospect of a steady career path. Companies, in turn, provided a structured environment with predictable work hours, which helped employees balance their professional and personal lives. However, this model is increasingly viewed as restrictive by the newer workforce--the younger generations.

The 9-to-5 workday originated during the Industrial Revolution and was created to optimize productivity in manufacturing settings where output was closely linked to the number of hours spent in the factory.

Yet, this rigid framework is becoming increasingly outdated in today's knowledge-driven economy. Contemporary jobs often revolve around project-based tasks with variable demands, rendering the traditional 9-to-5 more or less obsolete.

Productivity metrics have transformed significantly, with results no longer directly tied to 9 hours at a desk.

In contrast, Millennials and Gen Z face a vastly different economic landscape. Many of them view traditional 9-to-5 jobs as inadequate for meeting their financial needs and personal aspirations. With the cost of living rising and wages not always keeping pace, these younger generations often find the rigid work hours and limited flexibility of conventional office jobs less appealing.

The advent of the internet, mobile technology, and cloud computing has fundamentally transformed the way and location of work. Advances in remote work technologies and digital collaboration tools now allow many tasks to be completed virtually anywhere and anytime.

This newfound flexibility undermines the traditional 9-to-5 office-based workday. With the ability to access work resources, communicate with team members, and complete tasks remotely, younger generations increasingly question the need for a rigid 9-to-5 schedule.

The gig economy has seen remarkable expansion over the past decade, driven by platforms such as Uber, Airbnb, and a range of freelance websites that have popularized flexible work options. This shift provides the younger generations unparalleled autonomy over their work schedules and career trajectories, allowing them to choose projects and set hours that best fit their needs and preferences.

Recent data highlights the magnitude of this trend: by 2023, over half (52%) of the U.S. workforce had participated in the gig economy or engaged in independent work at some stage of their careers.

The gig economy presents several notable advantages. For one, it offers significant flexibility, enabling workers to balance multiple jobs, pursue side projects, or manage personal commitments with greater ease. Additionally, it provides opportunities for diverse income streams, allowing young people to capitalize on various skills and interests, potentially increasing their overall earnings.

However, there are also notable drawbacks. Gig workers often face income instability, as their earnings can fluctuate based on the availability of work and demand. This lack of financial predictability can make budgeting and long-term financial planning challenging. Moreover, gig workers generally lack traditional employment benefits, such as health insurance, retirement plans, and paid leave, which are typically provided in full-time jobs. This absence of benefits can lead to additional stress and financial burdens.

A recent study conducted by Qualtrics for Intuit Credit Karma reveals a significant shift in the perceptions of Gen Z U.S. adults aged 18 and older. According to the study, 60% of this demographic view traditional 9-to-5 jobs as unfulfilling and draining, while 43% express a strong disinterest in pursuing such positions altogether.

This changing perspective is compelling employers to rethink their work arrangements to attract and retain top talent from this generation.

Organizations that provide flexible work schedules and remote work options are increasingly seen as more appealing employers by younger workers. Companies adapting to these preferences can better meet the expectations of Gen Z, fostering a more engaged and motivated workforce.

Furthermore, globalization is a major reason behind the shifting norms in workforce culture across the world. As companies extend their reach across the globe, the traditional notion of a standard workday is increasingly becoming outdated. Operating in multiple time zones necessitates a level of flexibility that allows businesses to manage their global operations effectively. This has resulted in a shift toward varied working hours and a greater emphasis on asynchronous communication to accommodate different regional schedules.

This global perspective challenges the conventional 9-to-5 work framework, advocating for a more adaptable approach to scheduling that aligns with project demands and international collaboration. Instead of adhering to a rigid timeframe, work hours are now more fluid and tailored to support diverse time zones and dynamic project requirements. This evolution not only reflects the needs of a global workforce but also enhances productivity by allowing teams to work across different time zones seamlessly.

Perceptions about job security over the past few decades have shifted as well. The era of securing a job with a single company for 30 or 40 years and retiring with a solid pension is becoming a thing of the past. Today's workers are less inclined to spend their entire careers with one employer. Job hopping has become increasingly prevalent, especially in the wake of the pandemic. As a result, frequently changing jobs is no longer viewed negatively. Recruiters now understand that younger employees often embrace an entrepreneurial mindset. When encountering candidates with varied job histories, they are more likely to inquire about their career choices rather than focus on the length of time spent in each position.

Furthermore, Declining corporate loyalty toward employees is a thing of the modern world. In the past, hard work and dedication were often met with rewards, promotions, and job security. However, this is no longer the norm. Unlike companies such as Torani, which has maintained stability for a century without layoffs, many modern organizations are taking a different approach. The tech industry, in particular, has seen some of the largest layoffs, with 949 companies cutting over 200,000 jobs since January 2023. Similarly, Tyson Foods, a major player in the meat industry, reduced its senior leadership positions by about 15% and cut 10% of its corporate roles. With increasing layoffs and the rise of remote work, it's no wonder that job hopping is becoming more common.

The pandemic significantly reshaped people's values and expectations. Workers are now seeking roles that provide genuine fulfillment and recognition as individuals rather than mere job functions. Despite 82% of employees emphasizing the importance of being viewed as people by their organizations, only 45% feel their company actually meets this expectation, according to Gartner research. Additionally, employees are increasingly prioritizing flexibility in their work arrangements—encompassing when, where, and how they work. In contrast, many employers are enforcing return-to-office policies, leading to growing discontent among workers. This dissatisfaction drives job hopping in younger generations as these young employees search for positions that better align with their goals.

Nevertheless, In contemporary workplaces, it is common to find employees from up to four different generations working side by side. Each generation brings its own distinct style, needs, goals, and characteristics, which employers must navigate and accommodate.

It is now common knowledge that when multiple generations work together, their varying perspectives and work styles can lead to significant workplace conflicts. Older generations, such as Baby Boomers and Gen X, often value structure, hierarchy, and long-term commitment, viewing traditional methods and face-to-face communication as essential. In contrast, Millennials and Gen Z tend to prioritize flexibility, technology-driven communication, and rapid feedback, as mentioned in the previous chapters. These differing approaches can create friction; for example, older employees may perceive younger workers' preference for informal communication and quick decision-making as unprofessional or lacking commitment, while younger employees may find the older generation's reliance on formal procedures and hierarchical decision-making as cumbersome and outdated.

Furthermore, technological proficiency and attitudes toward authority further exacerbate these generational tensions. Older workers might struggle with or resist new technologies, while younger employees are often quick to embrace digital tools and innovative practices. This technological divide can lead to misunderstandings and inefficiencies. Additionally, differing views on work-life balance and career expectations—where older generations may value long hours and career advancement, and younger generations seek better work-life integration and flexible schedules—can result in disagreements over work norms and practices. Addressing these conflicts requires fostering open dialogue, encouraging mutual respect, and creating inclusive policies that accommodate diverse needs and preferences.

Recently, many contemporary corporations have focused on designing work environments that embrace and utilize the strengths of all four generations. These organizations understand the benefits of a diverse workforce and are adopting strategies to promote inclusivity and enhance collaboration among different age groups. Google now fosters cross-generational collaboration through mentorship programs and team-building activities, supporting diverse perspectives. The company emphasizes flexible work arrangements and continuous learning and caters to various work styles, helping employees from all generations thrive. Other companies like IBM also offer flexible schedules, remote work options, and continuous development opportunities for a multi-generational workforce. Its reverse mentoring program encourages younger employees to guide senior staff on technology and trends, which helps enhance intergenerational learning. Unilever is also one of the great examples of very few companies that have taken the initiative to create a conducive environment for a diverse workforce with flexible work arrangements and a focus on work-life balance. The company's development programs are designed to meet the needs of both younger and older employees, facilitating career growth and role transitions.

These examples illustrate how companies are integrating multiple generations by emphasizing flexibility, learning, and collaboration to address diverse employee needs in the highly globalized and technologically advanced world.

Despite the promising potential of technological advancements, a significant and pressing concern for younger generations is the rapid pace at which technology, particularly AI, is advancing. There is a growing apprehension that these technologies could potentially displace jobs at an alarming rate, often before individuals have the opportunity to adapt or upskill. Globally, there is increasing anxiety about how AI will reshape the job market and the implications this will have for coming generations. As technology evolves faster than the development of new skills, young people may face increasingly challenging economic conditions. This scenario underscores the urgency for proactive strategies to prepare for an uncertain future, emphasizing the need for ongoing education and adaptability to manage careers in an era where technological advancements continuously redefine the job landscape.

In "21 Lessons for the 21st Century," Yuval Noah Harari explores how artificial intelligence (AI) is expected to reshape the job market and influence career paths for future generations. Harari highlights the impact of AI and automation on the job market, noting that many routine and repetitive tasks across various industries are increasingly susceptible to being automated. Jobs with predictable patterns, such as those in manufacturing or administrative roles, are particularly vulnerable. This shift towards automation could result in significant job displacement, as tasks that are easily codified and mechanized are taken over by machines. As a result, many workers may find their roles obsolete, leading to substantial changes in employment landscapes.

Despite the potential for job displacement, Harari also emphasizes that AI could create entirely new job categories and industries that we currently cannot fully predict. This echoes past technological revolutions that led to the emergence of new professions and fields. For future generations, this means career paths will likely become more dynamic and require ongoing adaptation and learning. To navigate these changes, there will be a growing need for reskilling and lifelong learning, focusing on skills that AI cannot easily replicate, such as creative problem-solving and emotional intelligence. Additionally, the author pointed out concerns about increased inequality and job market polarization, where high-skill jobs become more lucrative while low-skill jobs become more precarious. Addressing these issues will be crucial for ensuring equitable opportunities and redefining work in a way that aligns with individual passions and values, moving beyond traditional employment notions.

Overall, AI is anticipated to present both challenges and opportunities in the job market. The future will demand adaptability, continuous learning, and a reevaluation of work structures and values. For younger and future generations, this means gearing up for a career environment that will consistently evolve, emphasizing the need for skills that complement and enhance human abilities in tandem with technological progress.

— Chapter 9 —
Values Vault - From "Get Off My Lawn" to "Save the Planet"

Psychological research from both early and contemporary scholars has consistently demonstrated that the environment in which individuals are raised—specifically, the experiences of deprivation or scarcity during childhood—significantly impacts their value systems in adulthood. The absence of certain elements in formative years can shape one's priorities, beliefs, and attitudes later in life.

So, how does this interplay between upbringing and values affect the modern workplace, and what role do employers play? Each generation's unique formative experiences, shaped by the prevailing social, political, and technological contexts, lead to distinct workplace values and expectations. For instance, Baby Boomers who experienced post-war stability often prioritize job security and long-term commitment. According to LiveAbout.com, the Baby Boomer generation is usually characterized by a set of workplace values and attitudes that include a strong focus on work, a tendency towards workaholism, and a high degree of independence and self-assertiveness. They are typically goal-oriented, career-driven, competitive, and committed to self-actualization. Collectively, these traits indicate a generation that values productivity and effectiveness at work, often placing work at the core of their lives, sometimes at the expense of maintaining a work-life balance.

Generation X, the cohort succeeding the Baby Boomers, marked a significant departure from the work-centric ethos of their predecessors. Growing up amidst the early stages of technological evolution, rapid socio-political transformations, and often limited adult oversight, Gen Xers developed a distinct set of values. This environment nurtured a generation characterized by heightened independence and adaptability, as they were accustomed to managing with minimal guidance and adjusting to swift changes.

In contrast to the Baby Boomers' focus on work, Gen Xers emphasize achieving a balanced life, embracing a "work hard, play hard" philosophy. As noted by Indeed, their key workplace values include a strong sense of independence and self-reliance, a commitment to maintaining a healthy work-life balance, flexibility, and a preference for informal work environments. This generation also values technological innovation and creativity, reflecting their upbringing during a period of significant digital transition.

Generation Y, commonly known as Millennials, follows Generation X and precedes Generation Z. As the largest generation in today's workforce, making up about 35% according to the U.S. Bureau of Labor Statistics, their upbringing and values are crucial for employers to understand. Raised during the transition to a fully digital world and impacted by significant events like 9/11, Millennials witnessed rapid technological advancements and the emphasis on work-life balance established by Gen X. This background has shaped a generation that values work environments aligning with their moral and socio-political beliefs, often prioritizing purpose over pay. Millennials are known for their emphasis on meaningful work, frequent and personalized communication, diversity, flexibility, teamwork, and continuous professional development.

Finally, Generation Z, now entering the workforce, represents a significant shift in both demographic and digital landscapes. Comprising 30% of the global population and set to make up a similar share of the workforce within five years, Gen Z is the first generation raised entirely in a digital world. Unlike previous generations, they grew up with instant access to social media and the internet, making them the "first global generation" with unparalleled exposure to diverse perspectives and global issues. Their experiences with economic instability, climate change, and the COVID-19 pandemic have shaped them into a cohort that values openness, connectivity, and a global sense of community, contrasting sharply with the more isolated experiences of earlier generations. Zurich and McKinsey & Company describe Generation Z as a cohort deeply committed to uncovering fundamental truths, exploring new possibilities, and redefining personal identity. This generation is characterized by a relentless pursuit of authenticity and a desire to break free from restrictive labels that might hinder their exploration of these deeper truths.

Furthermore, Younger generations tend to be more socio-culturally liberal than older ones, mainly because they grew up in safer and more prosperous environments. Research by Inglehart suggests that each generation develops different values based on the economic conditions during their formative years. Older generations, who faced economic hardships in their youth, often lean towards cultural conservatism and focus on distributional issues. In contrast, younger generations, raised during times of economic growth, emphasize individualism, personal freedom, and cultural liberalism.

In Western Europe, economic security hasn't grown as rapidly in recent decades as it did after World War II, which has reduced the differences in attitudes between post-war generations. Scholars have noted that generational differences in socio-cultural attitudes are crucial, as they reflect the broader social context of one's youth, compared to lifecycle effects, which are changes that occur within any generation over time. Thus, understanding generational values involves considering the economic and social conditions prevalent during each generation's adolescence.

The ideological divide between older and younger generations is increasingly shaping political dynamics and creating significant friction across various sectors. Older, more conservative generations often align with traditional, right-leaning policies emphasizing stability, traditional values, and limited government intervention. In contrast, younger generations, including Millennials and Generation Z, tend to support progressive, liberal policies advocated by the far left, focusing on social justice, environmental sustainability, and expansive social programs.

This generational split is not only reshaping the political landscape but also causing tensions within families. Parents from the Baby Boomer and Generation X cohorts may find themselves at odds with their Millennial and Gen Z children over political and social issues. These differences reflect broader societal shifts, where evolving values and priorities between generations create challenges in finding common ground. As these ideological conflicts continue to grow, they are influencing political discourse and decision-making on a global scale, highlighting the deepening divide between conservative and liberal viewpoints across generations.

Moreover, there is significant contention regarding climate change, with a notable disconnect between older generations and the urgent concerns of younger ones. Many older individuals seem largely indifferent to the fact that their actions have significantly contributed to the current climate crisis. This detachment is exacerbated by the reluctance or outright denial among some to acknowledge global warming as a severe and imminent threat. This denial, coupled with a lack of substantial efforts to reverse the damage already inflicted, is creating profound frustration among younger generations, who are increasingly worried about inheriting an unstable and deteriorating environment.

The refusal to address or even recognize the scale of climate change undermines current environmental efforts and jeopardizes the future well-being of upcoming generations. As younger people face the tangible consequences of environmental neglect and the growing instability of our planet, they are calling for urgent and comprehensive action to mitigate the damage and prevent further deterioration. This generational clash highlights a broader struggle between addressing long-term environmental sustainability and immediate, often conflicting, priorities.

While there are numerous differences in how generations approach various issues, not all examples are the same. Nonetheless, many instances of collaboration between older and younger generations have led to remarkable technological advancements and the emergence of new industries.

Intergenerational collaborations have often led to positive change by harnessing diverse perspectives and experiences to address complex challenges. For instance, the partnership between Baby Boomers and Millennials in the field of technology has been highly productive. Baby Boomers, with their extensive industry experience and historical knowledge, work alongside Millennials, who bring fresh digital skills and innovative thinking. This synergy has led to advancements in user-friendly technology and digital platforms. A notable example is the development of accessible tech tools and apps for seniors, combining the tech-savvy of younger generations with the insights and needs of older adults. This collaboration ensures that technology benefits all age groups, enhancing quality of life and bridging the digital divide.

In social justice, intergenerational teamwork has proven highly effective. The climate movement exemplifies this, with seasoned environmentalists-

-considered anomalies by their own generations--now working alongside passionate young activists like Greta Thunberg. The combination of the older generation's extensive experience with the younger generation's innovative approaches has strengthened advocacy efforts, leading to impactful global movements such as Fridays for Future and influential policy discussions. This collaboration blends historical insight with fresh perspectives, ensuring a cohesive and dynamic approach to addressing climate issues in the coming days. Notwithstanding, to bridge generational value divides while maintaining one's beliefs, strategic communication is key. Emphasizing shared goals is one effective strategy. For example, Baby Boomers may value job security in the workplace, while Millennials and Gen Z prioritize flexibility. By focusing on common objectives, such as boosting employee satisfaction and productivity, companies can find common ground that honors diverse values and work towards mutual success.

Fostering open dialogue and mutual respect is another effective approach. Creating spaces for all generations to share perspectives without judgment, such as through intergenerational mentorship programs like those at IBM, helps build understanding. Older employees offer experience and context, while younger ones provide fresh insights and tech expertise. This exchange promotes appreciation of diverse viewpoints and helps find common areas to work together.

Finally, adopting flexible solutions that address diverse preferences can bridge generational divides. For instance, in education, teachers can blend traditional methods with modern technology to meet the needs of students from various age groups. While some students excel with conventional techniques, others benefit from digital tools and interactive learning. By incorporating both approaches, educators honor different learning styles and values, ensuring effective education for everyone. This strategy demonstrates how flexibility and compromise can harmonize differing viewpoints without requiring the abandonment of core principles.

The shift in generational values reflects a dramatic transformation from past priorities to contemporary concerns. Older generations, like the Baby Boomers, often focused on personal achievement and work ethic, exemplified by a "Get Off My Lawn" mentality, emphasizing hard work and personal space. In contrast, younger generations, such as Millennials and Generation Z, are increasingly oriented towards broader social and environmental issues, adopting a "Save the Planet" mindset.

This shift highlights a move from individualistic and career-centric values to collective and ethical concerns, with newer generations prioritizing sustainability, inclusivity, and social responsibility, reflecting their upbringing in a rapidly evolving, interconnected world.

— Part III —
KUMBAYA, MY GEN

— Chapter 10 —
LOST IN TRANSLATION - THE GEN-Z TO BOOMER DICTIONARY

Language is very complex. It changes frequently, particularly with generations, as they are exposed to different experiences. The biggest change in language can be seen through Gen Z. The exposure to the internet, and the easy access it gives to communicate with different people have meant that the way Gen Z uses language is very different from that of previous generations. It also creates words that can slowly lose meaning due to the communication barrier between Gen Z and other generations like Gen X and Baby Boomers.

As a result, the meanings of certain words and phrases may become obscure or diluted over time, creating communication barriers between Gen Z and older generations. For example, terms that are widely understood within Gen Z might be less clear or even confusing to those unfamiliar with the latest online trends. This generational gap highlights how technological advancements and changing communication platforms can reshape language, making it a dynamic and ever-evolving aspect of human interaction.

A clear example of this linguistic evolution can be seen in the term "woke," which has gained prominence with Gen Z's heightened focus on social justice issues like equality and climate change. Originally, "woke" referred to being aware and actively engaged with important social issues and injustices. However, in recent times, the term has broadened and is often misused to describe a wide range of social conversations, sometimes generating generational friction.

As a result, "woke" has increasingly been used pejoratively, leading to negative stereotypes about Gen Z. A quick online search reveals numerous articles that use "woke" as an insult directed at Gen Z and their progressive views. Ironically, while the term was intended to reflect awareness and advocacy for social justice, it is now sometimes perceived as a derogatory label. This shift illustrates how language can become contentious and lead to misunderstandings between generations, highlighting the risks of misappropriating terms and the potential for reinforcing negative stereotypes.

The term "politically correct" has also changed in meaning over time. Originally, it was about following liberal views and avoiding language or actions that marginalize different groups. But recently, the term has become somewhat negative. It's often used to criticize media, comedy, and art, suggesting that being "politically correct" means being dull and overly conformist.

In reality, the concept shouldn't be seen as boring. Just like with the term "woke," it's important to be aware of how our language affects different generations. With the growing emphasis on age diversity, avoiding ageism can also be considered part of being "politically correct." Therefore, there's no reason to view being "politically correct" as a problem.

Trends can significantly influence language, leading to the creation of new expressions. A notable example from 2019 is the phrase "Ok Boomer." This term emerged as a retort to the negative stereotypes and criticisms often directed at younger generations by older ones. It acts as a digital dismissal, reflecting frustration and a desire to reject outdated perceptions.

Conversely, older generations also use language that may not resonate with younger people. For instance, terms like "workaholic," which was coined to describe the Baby Boomers' intense work ethic, may now seem outdated. Similarly, Baby Boomer slang such as "threads" (for clothes), "groovy" (for something cool), and "moo juice" (for milk) are largely forgotten by younger generations. While these examples are light-hearted, they highlight a broader issue: language evolves so rapidly that basic conversations between generations can become confusing or amusing.

Today, slang spreads rapidly thanks to the power of social media. With TikTok reaching over a billion monthly users by 2021, Gen Z quickly learns the latest szlang through viral videos. This new language doesn't need to wait for word of mouth, newspapers, or TV shows to catch on. Instead, young people born in the late '90s and early 2000s get immediate access to trending words and phrases directly from their phones.

A recent Forrester study highlights TikTok's popularity among teens, with 63% of 12-to-17-year-olds using it every week. This frequency surpasses that of Snapchat and Instagram, making TikTok the most influential platform for slang among younger users, with only YouTube having a larger reach.

Here's a humorous example of how generational language differences can lead to funny misunderstandings. Imagine a Baby Boomer at a family gathering, trying to stay hip with the younger crowd. While chatting with their Millennial granddaughter, the conversation takes a juicy turn, and she casually says, "Oh, come on, spill the tea!"

The Boomer, eager to show they're in touch with current slang, thinks it's a literal request. So, they grab a teapot and start pouring tea all over the table, bewildered as everyone looks on in confusion and laughter. The granddaughter, trying to explain through her giggles, says that "spill the tea" actually means to share gossip or juicy details, not to literally spill a beverage.

This funny mix-up underscores how quickly language evolves and how easy it is for different generations to misinterpret each other's phrases. With slang changing so rapidly, it's no surprise that well-meaning Boomers might find themselves unintentionally creating a mess while trying to keep up with the latest trends!

In a business setting, communication issues between generations can reduce productivity. Younger employees might feel misunderstood by older colleagues, while older workers might think younger employees are disrespectful. These misunderstandings can lead to increased conflict within teams, especially as media portrayals often exaggerate generational differences and misunderstandings.

To bridge the generational gap, starting with open conversations can be very effective. Communicating with colleagues from different age groups and learning about their perspectives can significantly reduce confusion and prevent conflicts. This could involve casual meetings over coffee or informal chats in the breakroom, which not only help clear up misunderstandings but also improve relationships and team dynamics.

To address communication gaps and reduce tension caused by language differences between generations, a practical approach is to familiarize oneself with the trendy terms favored by Gen Z. Understanding the meaning behind these modern phrases can help older generations better connect with younger individuals, even if they don't use the same slang themselves. This effort can go a long way in bridging the communication divide and fostering mutual respect.

Gen Z, while not necessarily expecting their parents to adopt their language, would appreciate the effort to understand it. This effort shows a willingness to connect and engage with the younger generation on their terms, which can significantly reduce misunderstandings. By learning the context and usage of contemporary slang, older generations can avoid misinterpreting or dismissing the meanings behind these terms.

Parents from Gen X and older Millennials who have children in Gen Z and Gen Alpha are increasingly making an effort to grasp the latest lingo. This endeavor not only enhances their ability to communicate more effectively with their kids but also helps in reducing potential conflicts and improving overall family dynamics. Engaging with current language trends is a practical way to bridge generational divides, making interactions smoother and fostering better understanding across age groups.

It would not be wrong to say that it goes both ways; Older and younger generations need to show willingness and the desire to learn about the ways that can make communication easier for everyone. When individuals from different generations make an effort to understand and appreciate each other's unique linguistic styles, it opens the door to more engaging and relatable conversations. For instance, when older generations take the time to learn and recognize modern slang, like FOMO (fear of missing out), No Cap(confirming one is not lying), and Drip (which refers to something stylish or style), etc., commonly used by the younger generations these days, they can better connect with their younger counterparts, showing that they value and respect their experiences and perspectives.

Conversely, when younger individuals show an interest in the language and expressions of older generations, who had their own slang when they were young, like threads (which means dress/style), and groovy (something fun, exciting), bummer (equivalent to Big Yikes for boomers), it demonstrates a willingness to bridge gaps and respect and context that comes with those terms. This mutual effort not only improves understanding but also enriches conversations by incorporating diverse viewpoints and experiences. Such interactions can lead to more enjoyable and fun discussions where each party feels heard and appreciated.

Overall, embracing these generational language differences encourages more genuine dialogue, reduces misunderstandings, and builds stronger relationships. By valuing and learning from each other's linguistic backgrounds, people from different age groups can create more inclusive and dynamic conversations, leading to greater empathy and connection across generations.

— Chapter 11 —
FAMILY FEUD - HOLIDAY EDITION

Family dynamics are inherently complex and convoluted for almost everyone. There might be very few people on this planet who do not struggle to maintain healthy ties with their families. However, the same can not be said for everyone. These are the connections people have with other people that they didn't choose but are bound by blood rather than shared values or interests. Consequently, it's natural for misunderstandings, disagreements, and even conflicts to arise, particularly between different generations.

In today's world, these generational divides are more pronounced due to the rapid pace of change and evolving societal norms. Modern challenges, such as technological advances and shifting cultural values, can exacerbate these tensions. Despite these hurdles, it's important to recognize that there are still many commonalities that unite people across generational lines.

It is happening for the first time in history that it has become common for great-grandparents to meet their great-grandchildren, with some families spanning four or even five generations alive at the same time. This multi-generational presence, while remarkable, can complicate family dynamics, especially when decision-making involves so many diverse viewpoints. Researchers have come up with the conclusion that age is a key factor in differences in behavior and attitudes, impacting everything from social policy to international relations.

The prospect of living to 100, though thrilling, brings its own set of challenges. Many individuals find themselves "sandwiched" between generations, juggling the responsibilities of raising their own children while simultaneously caring for aging parents. This unique situation adds another layer of complexity to family interactions and decision-making, reflecting both the benefits and burdens of extended lifespans.

Extended lifespans are reshaping how power, wealth, and decision-making are passed down through generations. With older generations maintaining control well into their 80s or even 90s, younger generations may find themselves waiting decades before they can assume leadership roles or influence key decisions. This extended period of waiting can be frustrating for those in their 60s who feel they are still in their prime, waiting for their chance to lead.

At the same time, younger family members, often in their 30s or 40s, are eager to step up and have their voices heard. They may feel ready and even entitled to contribute more significantly, seeing themselves as capable of taking on greater responsibilities. This creates a complex emotional landscape for their parents, who are caught between empathy for the younger generation's impatience and a natural reluctance to give up their hard-won authority. The balancing act between maintaining control and transitioning power highlights the evolving challenges of multigenerational family dynamics in an era of longer lifespans.

Furthermore, recent times have seen increased clashes between older and younger generations over political differences. The divide is particularly evident in discussions about social policies and reforms. Older generations, who may have grown up with more conservative or traditional viewpoints, often advocate for maintaining established systems and values. In contrast, younger generations, influenced by contemporary issues and a more progressive outlook, push for sweeping changes on topics like climate action, racial equality, and economic reform. These contrasting perspectives can lead to intense debates during family gatherings, where political discussions can quickly become contentious. Such differences highlight how evolving societal norms and values can impact family dynamics, often amplifying generational divides.

Rapid advancements in technology have significantly reshaped intergenerational relationships. The pervasive use of cell phones and social media has transformed communication, creating new ways in which information is shared and consumed. In the past, news was largely disseminated through traditional media with fewer sources, which helped maintain a certain level of shared understanding across generations.

Today, the explosion of digital platforms and opinion-driven content can intensify generational conflicts, as differing perspectives on information and technology can highlight and exacerbate existing value divides.

While social media and cell phones themselves are not inherently disruptive, they influence how generational values and conflicts come to the fore. Historically, younger generations have always sought to assert their independence from their parents, but technology amplifies these tendencies by providing new platforms for self-expression and rebellion. The impact of these technologies lies not in their existence but in how they alter the ways in which values are communicated and perceived, making generational clashes more pronounced.

While families often prioritize the importance of their relationships above all else, it can be challenging to remain composed when faced with strong opposing viewpoints. To foster harmony during family gatherings, one effective strategy is to establish agreements that promote mutual respect. For example, families might agree to "keep political and religious discussions off the table" to avoid heated debates and preserve the overall harmony of the gathering. This commitment helps ensure that disagreements do not overshadow the value of their relationships.

Additionally, families can implement other agreements to create a more inclusive environment. Setting boundaries around topics of discussion, such as agreeing to focus on shared interests or positive experiences, can help reduce tension.

Although seemingly minor, differences in communication preferences and age-based stereotypes can significantly affect relationships. Addressing these issues requires understanding each other's perspectives and preferences. For instance, a simple question like, "Do you prefer I call you on FaceTime, or would you rather I text first to check if you're available?" can clarify these preferences and help find a compromise that works for everyone.

Finding common ground can be straightforward, and many families have successfully navigated these differences by using shared communication tools. For example, some families set up group chats on platforms like WhatsApp or Snapchat, where younger family members teach older ones how to use the technology and vice versa. This exchange not only improves communication but also strengthens bonds by bridging generational gaps.

Imagine a world where generational tensions are not only addressed but embraced as opportunities for growth rather than exacerbated by misunderstanding and mistrust. It is entirely possible to envision such a world, and we believe it is essential for the well-being of families and society as a whole. Open dialogue and mutual respect can transform these tensions into valuable learning experiences and deepen familial bonds.

Generational conflicts are a universal experience, affecting families of all financial backgrounds. These conflicts are a natural part of relationships and can even be beneficial, as they often stem from genuine care and concern. The real danger lies in apathy, where a lack of engagement and communication can erode connections and prevent resolution. Embracing these challenges and working through them with understanding can lead to stronger, more resilient family relationships and a more empathetic society.

The secret to navigating generational differences effectively lies in focusing on what truly matters. Most families share a common goal: they want each member to find happiness and success while ensuring the well-being of the family unit as a whole. It's important to recognize that flourishing means different things to different people, and understanding this diversity can strengthen family bonds.

To enhance relationships and move beyond minor generational disagreements, families can adopt several strategies. Prioritizing quality time together is crucial; shared activities, such as family dinners, game nights, or collaborative projects, help bridge gaps and create lasting memories. Open communication is also key—creating regular opportunities for family members to express their thoughts and feelings in a supportive environment can reduce misunderstandings. Additionally, celebrating each person's unique strengths and perspectives fosters mutual respect and appreciation. By emphasizing common values and supporting each other's individual goals, families can build stronger, more harmonious relationships despite generational differences.

Achieving success in navigating generational differences often begins with a focus on commonalities rather than disparities. Building a shared understanding requires a commitment to remain open-minded and curious, avoiding hasty judgments or assumptions based on age or generational stereotypes. This means actively working to dismantle preconceived notions and recognizing that everyone, regardless of their generation, has valuable insights and experiences to offer.

Another essential component is fostering shared experiences that strengthen familial bonds beyond mere legal or financial ties. This involves not only engaging in meaningful conversations but also establishing and upholding family traditions that everyone values. By creating opportunities for family members to connect through joint activities, celebrations, and rituals, families can build deeper, more personal connections. Respectful communication and mutual understanding serve as the bedrock of these relationships, ensuring that family unity is maintained despite generational differences. Ultimately, by emphasizing shared goals and embracing each other's perspectives, families can enhance their relationships and create a more cohesive and supportive environment for everyone involved.

— Chapter 12 —
WORKPLACE WIZARDRY - WHEN
MILLENNIALS MANAGE BOOMERS

Unlike their predecessors, who accepted traditional notions of authority and work ethic, Millennials and Gen Z are challenging workplace established norms and seeking to redefine work practices that have persisted for decades.

Younger workers are more outspoken about their opinions compared to previous generations and expect their perspectives to be acknowledged and acted upon. They're asking loudly for the things everyone wants and have not been conditioned to accept limitations or delays in achieving their goals. Consequently, they are less inclined to conform to traditional cultural expectations, such as waiting their turn or earning their place, and are more likely to prioritize their own needs over organizational harmony. If dissatisfied, they are also more inclined to leave their positions compared to older employees.

As discussed previously, Millennial and Gen-Z employees place a high value on finding meaning in their work. They reject being viewed merely as numbers or seats to fill; instead, they seek to believe in the significance of their contributions and their company's mission. They are prepared to work diligently towards meaningful goals and significant achievements. However, research in the workplace suggests that they are less inclined to "follow orders without context" or remain in environments that they find unfulfilling or disrespectful. While they do not necessarily need to be in leadership positions, they expect to be heard and treated respectfully. They are more open to following rules or restrictions if they understand the rationale behind them.

Today's younger generations are actively pursuing happiness as a central goal and expect their work experiences to contribute to this objective. This represents a significant departure from previous generations, for whom career norms were centered around climbing the corporate ladder to achieve status, power, and financial reward or enduring dissatisfaction at work to find fulfillment elsewhere in their personal lives. By intentionally adapting workplaces to align with the younger generations' desire for meaningful and satisfying experiences, organizations can create environments that not only meet the needs of younger employees but also enhance overall resilience and support for workers of all ages. Embracing this shift can foster a more engaged and motivated workforce, benefiting the entire organization.

There is an ongoing debate regarding which generation excels more in actual job performance and who might be perceived as lazy. This persistent conflict can create a challenging work environment for both younger and older employees. For the younger generation, it can be frustrating to navigate stereotypes and expectations that might undervalue their contributions or innovations. Meanwhile, the older generation may face difficulties adapting to new approaches and technologies, leading to perceptions of resistance to change. This dynamic not only strains intergenerational relations but also highlights unique challenges for older employees, who might struggle to balance their established work habits with the evolving trends of the modern workplace.

On the internet, there are numerous instances where people have anonymously shared their experiences and frustrations about what makes different generations challenging to work with. For example, someone from the older generation shared, "Differences? LOL. Nobody under the age of 30 wants to do any actual work. And before you all flame me and say, 'Nobody pays well enough,' maybe you should have focused on building a career instead of just taking a job you never wanted to do in the first place. There's zero work ethic among young people these days. And before you call me a boomer, I'm 48. I'm a Xennial; get your stereotypes correct... But you're probably too lazy to even do that."—Millennial Slayer.

While someone from the younger generation shared:

"Whatever toxicity dragged them up the ladder, they were determined to recreate that — while still standing at the top of the ladder, refusing to move. The people I hear complain about Gen Z the most are boomers because they are the Skeksi in The Dark Crystal chanting, 'I am still emperor' at every generation that's followed."—Anonymous.

This highlights the persistent tensions and differing viewpoints that various generations hold about one another. The anonymous online discussions reveal how deeply entrenched these conflicts are, shedding light on the diverse and often conflicting perceptions each generation has regarding the work habits, values, and expectations of others. Such exchanges underscore the broader struggle to reconcile these differences and foster a more cooperative and understanding workplace environment.

"I'm riding that Xennial line between two generations. What I love about my Gen Z coworkers is their determination to disrupt the toxic power dynamic that has polluted corporate and nonprofit life for decades. As someone who often had to work for boomers, their currency was primarily misery.

That's another example of someone from the younger generation voicing his concern on the internet. As Gen Z challenges existing stereotypes, older generations must adapt and become more flexible, making room for younger individuals.

When discussing the work ethic of younger generations, it's important to remember that today's workplace is diverse in terms of age. The modern workforce includes employees from all age groups, with many older generations also joining companies and working alongside younger colleagues in various roles, including junior executive positions. This demographic mix raises questions about how younger generations are managing and interacting with their older counterparts. How are younger leaders navigating the complexities of managing older employees, and what strategies are they employing to foster a positive and productive work environment across generational lines? Understanding these dynamics is crucial for creating a harmonious workplace where all employees, regardless of age, can contribute effectively and feel valued.

When younger generations take on managerial roles over older employees, they encounter unique challenges and opportunities that can significantly shape the workplace dynamics. One of the primary challenges is navigating the established norms and expectations that older employees bring with them. Older workers might have long-standing work habits and viewpoints that clash with the newer management style or innovative approaches introduced by younger leaders. This can lead to resistance or friction as both parties adjust to the evolving workplace culture.

On the flip side, younger managers have the opportunity to bring fresh perspectives and modern practices into the workplace. They often embrace technological advancements and contemporary work methods that can enhance efficiency and innovation. By integrating these new approaches, younger leaders can drive positive change and improve organizational performance. This can be particularly beneficial in industries undergoing rapid transformation or facing competitive pressures. However, it is crucial for younger managers to approach these opportunities with an understanding of the existing work environment, balancing new ideas with respect for the established practices and wisdom of their older counterparts.

As the workforce becomes more age-diverse, it's crucial for younger managers to master the skills needed to work effectively with older employees. With the pandemic subsiding and older workers re-entering the job market, many younger managers now find themselves overseeing colleagues who may be significantly older.

This scenario creates a distinct challenge that requires careful training and a profound understanding to build a positive and collaborative work environment. Here are several strategies and examples that can assist younger leaders in managing older colleagues with increased patience and respect.

A key element in managing older employees is promoting open communication. Younger managers should foster an environment where all employees feel comfortable sharing their thoughts and ideas. Avoiding age discrimination is vital, and HR should train managers to refrain from age-related questions and to treat everyone with respect. By encouraging transparent dialogue, younger managers can build trust and cultivate a positive work environment.

Effective team collaboration hinges on understanding and adapting to diverse communication preferences. Younger employees may favor digital platforms like Slack, while older employees might prefer traditional methods. Younger managers should accommodate these differences by providing training and support for various communication tools to ensure smooth and effective interactions.

Building strong relationships with older employees begins with finding common ground. Younger managers should make an effort to learn about their team members' backgrounds and interests. Platforms like LinkedIn can offer valuable insights into shared experiences. However, it's important to respect privacy and get permission before looking into personal details. By connecting over mutual interests, trust can grow, and teamwork can improve.

Older employees bring valuable experience and knowledge to the table. Younger managers should leverage this by actively seeking their feedback and input. By respecting and acknowledging their expertise, younger managers can foster a collaborative environment where older employees feel valued. Soliciting their insights on company growth and weaknesses can offer valuable perspectives and show appreciation for their contributions.

Many older employees are eager to keep learning and develop new skills. Younger managers can support this by offering learning opportunities and encouraging skill development. By asking older employees about their interests, managers can tailor development plans to their goals. Additionally, the experience and corporate knowledge of older employees are valuable resources. Younger managers should seek their guidance and advice before making decisions to benefit from their insights and avoid potential pitfalls.

Older employees might use different methods to achieve results compared to younger ones. Younger managers should foster an environment where diverse approaches are welcomed, allowing older employees to utilize their preferred methods and share unique perspectives. Nevertheless, Building trust is essential for a successful manager-employee relationship. Younger managers should act professionally, establish clear boundaries, and maintain a managerial dynamic rather than attempting to befriend their employees.

This collaborative dynamic not only enhances the work experience for everyone but also strengthens team cohesion and adaptability. By integrating the strengths of both younger and older generations, organizations can foster a more resilient and innovative environment. This synergy leads to a richer, more diverse workplace where varied perspectives drive creativity and problem-solving, ultimately contributing to overall organizational success and growth.

— Chapter 13 —
Digital Detox vs. Always On - Finding Balance in the Chaos

In today's rapidly evolving digital world, having access to technology and digital skills is crucial for engaging in contemporary society. Yet, there are noticeable differences in how various age groups embrace and use digital tools, with each generation showing different levels of ease and expertise. This narrative will explore the generational differences in technology use, examine the factors contributing to these gaps, and suggest ways to bridge them, promoting greater inclusivity in the digital age.

As previously noted, generational differences significantly influence individuals' attitudes toward and adoption of technology. The impact of these differences is evident across three key generations often discussed in the context of technology adoption:

Baby Boomers (born approximately 1946–1964) grew up during a period marked by rapid technological evolution, including the advent of personal computers and the internet. While many Baby Boomers have adapted to these changes and embraced technology, some may still encounter challenges. These difficulties often stem from limited exposure to digital tools earlier in their lives or a lack of formal training in using modern technology.

Generation X (born 1965–1980) experienced the rise of personal computing and the internet during their formative years. They were among the early adopters of email, mobile phones, and social media platforms. Generation X is generally comfortable with technology and has witnessed significant advancements firsthand.

Millennials (born 1981–1996) are often at the forefront of technology adoption and usage. Their comfort with technology surpasses that of older generations, a trend that remains strong today. Despite this, there has been notable progress in technology adoption among older generations since 2012, particularly among Generation X and Baby Boomers.

A recent Pew Research Center survey of U.S. adults conducted in early 2019 provides insight into these generational differences. It found that 93% of Millennials (ages 23 to 38 this year) own smartphones, compared to 90% of Generation Xers (ages 39 to 54 this year). In contrast, 68% of Baby Boomers (ages 55 to 73) and only 40% of the Silent Generation (ages 74 to 91) have adopted smartphone technology. This data highlights the evolving landscape of technology adoption across generations and underscores the varying degrees of technological integration among different age groups.

While Baby Boomers have increasingly embraced various technologies in recent years, the Silent Generation has been slower to follow suit. Only 40% of individuals from the Silent Generation report owning a smartphone, and an even smaller percentage—33%—own a tablet computer or use social media (28%). Previous surveys by the Pew Research Center have highlighted that older adults often encounter distinct challenges when adopting new technologies. These challenges include a lack of confidence in using new devices and physical difficulties in interacting with them.

The internet presents distinct advantages and disadvantages for different generations. For younger generations, such as Millennials and Gen Z, the internet is often seen as a powerful tool that has positively transformed society. A 2018 survey by the Center revealed that 73% of Millennials who use the internet believe it has had a largely beneficial impact on society. They appreciate the Internet for its role in facilitating communication, providing access to information, and enabling opportunities for personal and professional growth. However, they also face challenges related to issues like online privacy, cyberbullying, and the potential for digital addiction.

In contrast, older generations, including the Silent Generation, tend to view the internet's impact with more caution. According to the same survey, 63% of online users from the Silent Generation perceive the internet as having a mostly positive effect on society, though they may experience more skepticism or concern about its implications. These concerns often stem from issues such as digital literacy, the overwhelming amount of information available, and the potential for misinformation. While older users recognize the benefits of the internet, they may also encounter barriers related to adapting to new technologies and managing their digital interactions effectively.

The rise of artificial intelligence (AI) and other advanced technologies is generating apprehension across both younger and older generations. There is uncertainty about how these innovations will reshape the job market and their broader societal impacts in the future. In the summer of 2018, a survey of 979 technology pioneers, innovators, developers, business and policy leaders, researchers, and activists shed light on these concerns.

Experts predict that while networked AI will enhance human productivity, it also poses risks to human autonomy, agency, and capabilities. They foresee AI potentially matching or surpassing human intelligence in areas such as complex decision-making, reasoning, analytics, pattern recognition, visual and speech recognition, and language translation. These "smart" systems are expected to revolutionize various domains—saving time, reducing costs, improving safety, and providing personalized experiences across communities, transportation, infrastructure, agriculture, and business processes.

Optimistically, many experts highlighted AI's promising potential in healthcare, where it could transform patient diagnosis and treatment and assist elderly individuals in leading healthier lives. AI's ability to handle vast amounts of data could also advance public health initiatives and enhance education systems. However, despite these optimistic projections, experts have shared concerns about the long-term implications of AI on future generations.

In today's digitally saturated environment, many individuals are finding innovative ways to implement digital detox strategies while still staying connected to the modern world. Millennials, in particular, are in charge of adopting practices that limit social media usage to combat the mental strain and stress often associated with these platforms. These digital detox strategies involve creating boundaries for social media use, such as setting specific times for checking notifications or designating tech-free zones and times throughout the day. By doing so, they aim to reclaim their time and mental well-being, fostering a healthier balance between their online and offline lives.

The pressure of living up to the expectations set by a consumer-driven society has further motivated young people to seek out these digital detox methods. The relentless comparison of their lives to curated, idealized portrayals on social media can contribute to feelings of inadequacy and stress. Many millennials are recognizing the detrimental effects that constant exposure to such content can have on their self-esteem and overall mental health. As a response, they are increasingly turning to digital detox approaches to mitigate these negative impacts, aiming to cultivate a more authentic and fulfilling lifestyle that is less influenced by external pressures and unrealistic standards.

By engaging in digital detox, millennials are not completely disconnecting from modern technology but are instead striving to use it more mindfully. This conscious approach allows them to enjoy the benefits of digital connectivity without falling prey to the stressors that come with excessive social media use. Through strategies like scheduled breaks, app usage limits, and mindful consumption, they are working to enhance their quality of life and mental health. This shift reflects a growing awareness of the need for balance in a world where digital engagement is increasingly intertwined with personal and professional life.

Finding a healthy balance between staying connected and unplugging requires tailored strategies that align with the needs and preferences of different generations. For Millennials and Gen Z, who are deeply immersed in digital technology, research-based tips include using digital tools to set boundaries on screen time and social media usage. Studies show that apps like "Forest" or "Focus" can help manage and limit screen time effectively. A study in Computers in Human Behavior found that setting specific limits on social media use significantly reduced anxiety and depressive symptoms among young adults. Additionally, taking scheduled breaks from social media, as recommended in Cyberpsychology, Behavior, and Social Networking, has decreased stress and improved overall well-being.

For Generation X, balancing connectivity often involves establishing clear boundaries between work and personal life. Implementing tech-free zones in the home, such as designating certain areas for family time or relaxation, can reduce the strain of constant digital engagement. Research published in the Journal of Applied Social Psychology supports the idea that creating spaces free from technology can enhance family relationships and alleviate stress. Furthermore, setting aside specific times for checking work emails and social media can prevent burnout and improve work-life balance. A study in Occupational Health Psychology highlights that maintaining these boundaries helps reduce job-related stress and enhances overall productivity.

Baby Boomers and the Silent Generation may benefit from simpler technology strategies that enhance their digital experience without overwhelming them. For this group, establishing scheduled times for digital communication and limiting the use of complex technology can help manage stress. Research in Educational Gerontology suggests that simplifying technology use makes it more accessible and less intimidating for older adults. Additionally, prioritizing in-person interactions over digital communication can be especially beneficial. Moreover, according to The Journals of Gerontology, face-to-face social interactions contribute significantly to emotional well-being and reduce feelings of loneliness, providing a more meaningful and satisfying social experience.

Mindfulness techniques offer effective strategies for digital detox across generations, helping individuals manage stress and improve overall well-being. For younger generations, such as Millennials and Gen Z, techniques like mindful meditation apps can be particularly useful. Apps such as "Headspace" and "Calm" provide guided meditations and mindfulness exercises designed to help users unplug from their digital devices and center themselves in the present moment. Research published in The Journal of the American Medical Association shows that mindfulness meditation can reduce symptoms of anxiety and depression, which are often exacerbated by excessive digital engagement. By incorporating short, daily meditation sessions, younger people can create a buffer between their digital activities and their mental health, fostering a sense of calm and focus.

Older generations, including Baby Boomers and the Silent Generation, may benefit from mindful walking and nature engagement as a form of digital detox. Engaging in walks through natural settings allows for a break from screens while also providing physical exercise and exposure to nature, which has been shown to have calming effects. A study published in Environmental Science & Technology found that spending time in natural environments can significantly lower stress levels and improve mood. Older adults can incorporate mindful walking into their routine by focusing on their surroundings, sensations, and breathing, which helps them stay present and reduce reliance on digital devices.

Another effective technique for all age groups is mindful journaling, which involves writing down thoughts and feelings without digital interruptions. This practice can help individuals process their experiences and emotions in a structured, non-digital format. For younger generations, mindful journaling can serve as a way to reflect on their daily digital habits and set intentions for balanced screen time. For older adults, it provides a method to articulate thoughts and reduce stress without the need for digital tools. Research in The Journal of Clinical Psychology supports the benefits of journaling for mental health, including improved mood and reduced anxiety. By dedicating a few minutes each day to mindful journaling, people of all ages can achieve greater control and mindfulness in their lives.

— Part IV —
The Remix: Mashup Culture

— Chapter 14 —
GENERATIONAL FUSION - WHEN MILLENNIALS TEACH BOOMERS TO TIKTOK

When considering mentorship, many people often envision a scenario where a seasoned Baby Boomer imparts wisdom about office politics and career challenges accumulated over decades. However, there is a lesser-known but increasingly important form of mentorship known as "reverse mentoring." In reverse mentoring, junior employees take on the role of advisors, offering valuable insights and guidance to senior leaders. This approach focuses on emerging trends and developments, such as advancements in technology, as well as shifting societal and cultural norms. This dynamic not only facilitates a two-way exchange of knowledge but also helps bridge generational gaps within organizations.

In recent years, mentoring has evolved into a versatile tool for both personal and professional development. Among the various mentoring models, reverse mentoring has gained notable prominence. This innovative approach, which began to rise in popularity in the late 1990s, upends the traditional notion that knowledge and wisdom flow exclusively from senior to junior employees.

As Generation Z enters the workforce, workplaces now feature a blend of four different generations, each contributing its own unique experiences and insights.

Reverse mentoring is highly effective because it creates new opportunities for learning and knowledge-sharing that traditional mentoring often misses. By empowering junior employees to share their insights, this approach enriches the organization as a whole. It helps junior staff feel valued for their contributions while keeping senior employees updated on the latest social and technological trends.

This bottom-up model promotes cross-generational knowledge exchange, improves communication, and enhances understanding within the workplace. Senior leaders benefit from fresh perspectives on emerging trends, develop crucial digital skills, and contribute to a more inclusive culture that attracts and retains diverse talent. Reverse mentoring also addresses areas beyond technology, including diversity, inclusion, and breaking down generational stereotypes, leading to improved communication and mutual learning.

A fundamental principle of reverse mentoring is the acknowledgment that everyone possesses unique knowledge and skills that can drive collective growth. This approach fosters transparency, encourages open dialogue, and provides opportunities for personal and professional development for all involved.

Reverse mentoring has been embraced by organizations of all sizes, from large multinational corporations like Novartis to small startups with only a few team members. This approach provides organizations with a powerful tool for driving significant cultural changes by shifting communication channels in a less conventional direction.

Over time, older generations have increasingly embraced the digital habits of younger people. Many have warmed up to social media platforms such as Facebook and TikTok, discovering both enjoyment and a sense of connection through these channels. For instance, Baby Boomers and Gen Xers now actively participate in Facebook groups, share updates, and even post nostalgic content. On TikTok, they've been joining in on viral challenges and trends, often with amusing and heartwarming results.

These interactions frequently lead to funny and endearing encounters between the generations. Older users might share their creative attempts at popular dances or react to memes with a blend of curiosity and hilarity. Such moments not only highlight the bridging of digital divides but also foster intergenerational bonding as the older generation learns to navigate and appreciate the nuances of contemporary online culture alongside their younger counterparts.

The internet is brimming with examples of all four generations engaging in enjoyable online activities together.

In a delightful twist, many Baby Boomers have been jumping on TikTok to learn and perform viral dance routines. One standout example is a group of retirees who became TikTok sensations after mastering the "Renegade" dance. Their videos not only garnered millions of views but also inspired countless positive comments from younger generations, bridging the gap with laughter and shared joy.

On the flip side, Gen Z has been discovering the charm of vinyl records, often with a nostalgic nod to the music formats of previous decades. Young adults visit thrift stores and flea markets to build their vinyl collections and share their finds and experiences on social media. Some have even started Instagram accounts dedicated to their growing collections, blending retro aesthetics with modern digital culture.

A heartwarming trend involves Millennials helping Baby Boomers navigate the world of streaming services. Whether it's setting up Netflix, Hulu, or Disney+, younger family members are guiding their older relatives through the process. In turn, Boomers are sharing their favorite classic films and TV shows, leading to cozy movie nights and new shared interests.

Known for their adaptability, Gen Xers are now helping their older peers and parents get acquainted with video conferencing platforms like Zoom. Their guidance often covers everything from setting virtual backgrounds and sharing screens to using fun filters. This has led to a series of entertaining virtual meetings where tech hiccups turn into shared jokes, enhancing a sense of community.

Baby Boomers are also exploring the realm of internet memes, often with younger generations helping them navigate the latest trends. This playful interaction frequently leads to Boomers creating their own meme content, which, though sometimes amusingly out of sync with current trends, is always warmly embraced by their younger relatives.

Embracing new trends is fostering a gradual shift in understanding between older and younger generations. As older individuals engage with contemporary trends, they gain insight into the perspectives and interests of younger people. This process of learning and adaptation is not just about keeping up with the latest fads; it's about bridging generational gaps. The positive interactions that arise from this mutual exploration lead to a growing sense of respect and understanding across generational cohorts. By navigating these new cultural landscapes together, both sides are able to appreciate each other's viewpoints and experiences, ultimately strengthening intergenerational bonds.

Similarly, younger people who interact with older generations and observe their willingness to adapt and learn gain a more nuanced appreciation of their experiences and wisdom. This mutual exploration helps to dispel myths and assumptions, fostering a more nuanced and respectful view of each other. Through these meaningful interactions, both generations can appreciate the strengths and contributions of the other, leading to richer, more harmonious relationships and a more inclusive understanding of one another's perspectives.

Intergenerational interactions can significantly enhance cognitive functions in aging individuals by providing mental stimulation and fostering social engagement. When older adults engage with younger generations, they often participate in activities that require problem-solving, learning new technologies, or adapting to new trends. These activities challenge their cognitive abilities and encourage continuous mental activity, which is crucial for maintaining cognitive health. Studies have shown that social interaction and mental stimulation can delay the onset of cognitive decline and reduce the risk of neurodegenerative diseases like dementia and Alzheimer's. For example, research by the National Institute on Aging (2018) indicates that older adults who remain socially active and mentally engaged exhibit better cognitive performance and lower cognitive impairment.

Moreover, cross-generational learning offers unexpected benefits by creating a dynamic exchange of knowledge and perspectives that enriches the cognitive experiences of older adults. When younger people introduce new concepts or technologies to older individuals, it encourages them to think critically and adapt, which can enhance their cognitive flexibility and problem-solving skills. This interaction often leads to increased self-esteem and a sense of purpose, further supporting cognitive health. A study published in JAMA Network Open (2020) found that older adults who regularly engaged in activities involving younger people showed improvements in memory and cognitive function, highlighting the profound impact that these cross-generational exchanges can have on mental well-being.

Further research on this subject has highlighted the positive effects of interactions between aging older generations and empathetic younger individuals. For example, a study by Cuddy et al. (2015) found that engaging with younger generations can enhance cognitive vitality and social well-being among older adults, partly due to increased social interaction and emotional support.

The research also uncovered interesting trends in empathy over time. While earlier data showed stability in perspective-taking and empathic concern from 1979 to 1999, there was a notable decline from 2000 to 2007. However, from 2008 onwards, there was a marked resurgence in these empathetic traits among American undergraduates. This increase in empathy remained significant even after adjusting for various demographic, economic, and interpersonal factors. This trend suggests that, following a period of diminished empathic engagement, there has been a recent and substantial recovery in empathic concern and perspective-taking among younger people, which may contribute to the observed benefits for older adults.

Here is the graph that depicts the trends in empathy from younger generations towards older individuals over the years.

[Generation Empathy: The Surprising Surge of Compassion in Modern Youth | SPSP. (2024, July 26). https://spsp.org/news/character-and-context-blog/martingano-modern-youth-compassion-empathy-increase]

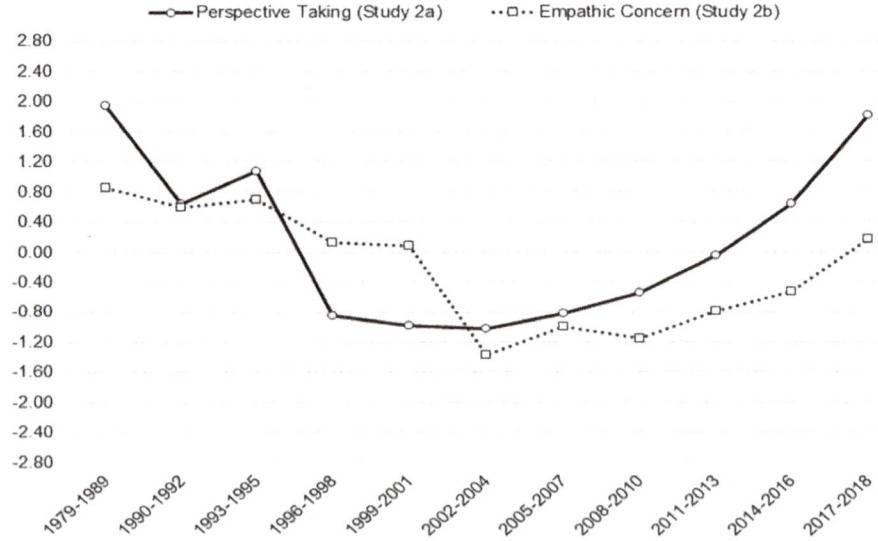

Facilitating skill swaps between different generations can be highly effective in various settings, such as family gatherings and corporate team-building exercises. For example, in family settings, organizing regular "tech tutorials" where younger family members teach older relatives how to use new devices or social media platforms can be both educational and bonding. This can be structured as casual workshops or one-on-one sessions, where younger individuals demonstrate skills like setting up video calls or navigating online resources. Similarly, in corporate environments, structured team-building exercises that pair younger employees with more experienced colleagues can be beneficial. For instance, reverse mentoring programs, mentioned above as well, where younger employees mentor senior staff on emerging technologies or social trends, foster mutual learning and respect. This exchange not only helps in skill development but also enhances team building at the workplace.

These skill exchanges offer several benefits to organizations and family dynamics. In corporate settings, they can lead to a more agile and innovative workforce. When younger employees share their tech-savvy skills and fresh perspectives, they can help streamline processes and introduce new approaches that benefit the organization. This cross-generational learning can also promote a culture of collaboration and adaptability, which is crucial in today's fast-evolving business landscape. Furthermore, when senior staff share their extensive experience and industry knowledge with younger colleagues, it can lead to improved decision-making and strategic planning.

At home, facilitating productive interactions between elders and younger family members can ease generational tensions and foster a more harmonious environment. By creating opportunities for mutual teaching and learning, family members can bridge gaps in understanding and build stronger relationships. Overall, such interactions not only improve interpersonal relationships but also enrich each generation's knowledge and perspectives, leading to a more cohesive and appreciative family dynamic.

— Chapter 15 —
INNOVATION NATION - HARNESSING MULTI-GEN SUPERPOWERS

Many managers acknowledge that having a diverse workforce can be advantageous for their organizations, yet demonstrating or quantifying these benefits, particularly in terms of how diversity influences a company's innovative capabilities, can be challenging.

Recent research, however, presents compelling evidence that diversity not only fosters innovation but also propels market growth. This insight underscores the importance of making concerted efforts to ensure that leadership teams not only reflect diverse perspectives but also actively leverage the strengths that come from these differences.

Understanding and valuing the different generations present in the workplace is essential for advancing diversity, equity, and inclusion (DEI) initiatives. Each generation contributes distinct perspectives, skills, and values that can greatly enhance an organization's cultural dynamics and operational effectiveness. While humor can sometimes alleviate tension during conflicts, relying on it alone is insufficient for fostering genuine inclusion and equity. In fact, such approaches might deepen divisions within teams rather than bridge gaps.

As the world enters 2024, people are beginning to see the emergence of the Alpha Generation in the workforce. Born in the early 2010s, this new cohort is poised to offer innovative insights and advanced digital proficiency, further diversifying and enriching the generational mix within organizations. Embracing the unique attributes of all generations will be key to leveraging their collective strengths and driving continued growth and cohesion.

Despite the challenges, a workforce comprised of multiple generations offers significant advantages. When a company's employees mirror the diversity of its customer base, it becomes easier to understand and cater to that demographic. For instance, insights from employees of different age groups can provide a clearer picture of the preferences and behaviors of various segments, enhancing marketing and customer service strategies.

Moreover, generational diversity creates valuable mentoring opportunities. Younger team members can introduce older colleagues to emerging technologies and trends through reverse mentoring, while experienced professionals can share their extensive industry knowledge with newer hires. This exchange of expertise boosts overall team proficiency and strengthens cohesion.

The diverse viewpoints and values each generation brings can also drive innovation. By addressing and embracing generational differences, companies can foster a collaborative environment that encourages creative problem-solving and leads to groundbreaking ideas.

Diversity creates a fertile environment for the exchange and fusion of ideas. When individuals from various backgrounds and areas of expertise collaborate, they introduce a range of perspectives and problem-solving approaches. This blend of viewpoints can ignite creative solutions to complex challenges. For example, in a product development project, a multidisciplinary team comprising engineers, designers, and marketers can leverage their diverse skill sets and insights. Engineers might focus on technical feasibility, designers could enhance the product's aesthetics and user experience, and marketers might offer valuable perspectives on consumer behavior and market trends. By integrating these varied contributions, the team can develop a more comprehensive and innovative product that addresses multiple aspects of the market and user needs.

As highlighted in earlier chapters, several companies have effectively integrated diversity into their workplaces, leading to substantial growth and establishing themselves as major players in today's market economy. Here are some notable examples:

Google stands out as a prime example of leveraging workforce diversity to drive innovation. The tech giant's commitment to fostering a varied team has led to the development of numerous groundbreaking products. For instance, Google's diverse teams contributed to the creation of products like

Google Search and Google Ads, which are the result of cross-disciplinary collaboration among engineers, designers, and marketing experts from different generational and cultural backgrounds. Google's emphasis on inclusivity has also facilitated creative solutions and ideas, helping the company remain at the forefront of technological advancements.

Procter & Gamble (P&G) is another company that has harnessed the power of a diverse workforce to achieve remarkable innovations. P&G's approach to multigenerational collaboration is evident in their development of products like the Swiffer and Tide Pods. By integrating insights from employees across different age groups and expertise areas—ranging from product development and design to consumer insights and marketing—P&G has created products that cater to a wide range of consumer needs. This inclusive approach has enabled P&G to continually refine its offerings and stay competitive in the fast-paced consumer goods market.

IBM exemplifies how a diverse workforce can lead to pioneering solutions in technology. IBM's commitment to diversity has been a driving force behind innovations such as IBM Watson, a cognitive computing system that uses artificial intelligence to analyze vast amounts of data. The success of Watson can be attributed to the collaborative efforts of IBM's employees, who come from various generational and professional backgrounds. This diversity has enabled IBM to integrate a wide range of perspectives and expertise, leading to breakthrough solutions in fields such as healthcare and finance. By embracing a broad spectrum of ideas and experiences, IBM has consistently pushed the boundaries of technological innovation.

So, to integrate strategies that promote inclusiveness and growth in the long run, companies need to adopt policies that ensure that. Creating environments that foster multigenerational creativity and collaboration requires a strategic approach that values the unique contributions of each generation while promoting open communication and mutual respect. One successful strategy is to implement structured mentoring programs that encourage knowledge sharing between younger and older employees or community members. For instance, reverse mentoring, explained in detail in the previous chapters, allows younger individuals to provide insights into new technologies and trends while seasoned professionals can offer their vast experience and industry knowledge. This reciprocal exchange bridges generational gaps and enhances overall skill development and innovation.

Another effective strategy involves creating inclusive spaces and practices that accommodate the needs and preferences of different age groups. In workplaces, this can mean offering flexible work arrangements that cater to varying life stages, such as remote work options for those balancing family commitments or flexible hours for older employees approaching retirement. In community settings, it might involve designing programs and events that appeal to a broad age range, ensuring that activities are accessible and engaging for everyone. By accommodating these diverse needs, organizations and communities can ensure that all generations feel valued and can contribute their unique perspectives.

Finally, fostering a culture of continuous learning and adaptability is crucial for nurturing multigenerational collaboration. Encouraging ongoing professional development and providing opportunities for all age groups to learn new skills helps keep the workforce dynamic and innovative. In workplaces, this can include regular training sessions, workshops, and learning platforms that cater to different learning styles and technological proficiencies. In community settings, offering diverse educational programs and collaborative projects can stimulate creativity and engagement across generations. By creating an environment that prioritizes learning and flexibility, organizations and communities can better harness the collective strengths of their multigenerational participants, driving forward innovation and creativity.

Looking into the future, the increasing emphasis on multiculturalism and diversity is poised to significantly drive innovation and modernize various aspects of society. One key aspect is the growing recognition of diverse perspectives as a catalyst for creativity and problem-solving. Multicultural and multigenerational teams bring together different cultural backgrounds, experiences, and viewpoints, which can lead to novel solutions and groundbreaking ideas. This diversity in thought is particularly crucial in a globalized economy, where businesses and organizations must cater to a wide range of markets and customer needs. As more companies and institutions embrace this diversity, people can expect a surge in innovative products and services that are better aligned with the varied preferences of a global audience.

The future of multigenerational innovation is also likely to be shaped by the integration of diverse age groups within collaborative environments.

As younger and older generations work together, they will combine their unique strengths—such as digital fluency from younger employees and extensive industry experience from older workers. This synergy can lead to the development of advanced technologies and solutions that address complex challenges. For example, in sectors like healthcare and technology, cross-generational teams might create more effective and user-friendly solutions by merging cutting-edge innovations with practical, time-tested knowledge. Such collaboration will foster a more dynamic and adaptive approach to problem-solving, driving progress in various fields.

Moreover, the trend towards greater multicultural and generational inclusivity is likely to accelerate the modernization of societal structures. This includes changes in how businesses operate, how communities are organized, and how policies are shaped. As diverse voices and experiences become integral to decision-making processes, we can anticipate more equitable and inclusive systems that better reflect and serve the needs of a diverse population. This evolution will contribute to a more interconnected and modern world, where innovation is driven by a broad spectrum of ideas and perspectives, ultimately leading to more sophisticated and adaptive solutions to global challenges.

— Chapter 16 —
THE GRAND FINALE - ORCHESTRATING THE SYMPHONY OF GENERATIONS

Generational diversity in the workplace has become increasingly common, with multiple age groups working together more than ever before. Embracing and understanding these generational differences is essential for creating a collaborative and effective team environment. The modern workforce is a blend of Baby Boomers, Generation X, Millennials, and Generation Z, each bringing distinct perspectives shaped by their unique life experiences and backgrounds. Recognizing and valuing these diverse viewpoints enhances communication and fosters a more inclusive workplace. Each generation contributes different skills and insights, and when leveraged properly, this diversity can lead to greater innovation and problem-solving capabilities. However, managing these generational differences can present challenges like varying communication styles and work expectations. It is crucial to cultivate an environment that promotes mutual respect, open dialogue, and understanding to bridge these gaps effectively. Following are some of the characteristics of each generation, the advantages of embracing generational diversity, and strategies for overcoming potential challenges to build stronger, more cohesive teams.

Each generation contributes distinct viewpoints, experiences, and working styles to the workplace, making it essential to understand these variations for cultivating a harmonious and effective team environment. Generational diversity encompasses the range of age groups present in a team or organization, from the Silent Generation to Generation Z. Each cohort has its own set of characteristics that influence their work habits and attitudes. As a leader, appreciating these generational differences is crucial for managing and inspiring a cohesive team.

One important factor in understanding generational diversity is recognizing the core values and priorities that drive each group. For instance, Baby Boomers, born between 1946 and 1964, often emphasize dedication, hard work, and personal interaction. In contrast, Millennials, born between 1981 and 1996, frequently value flexibility, work-life balance, and the integration of technology into their roles. By grasping these diverse values, leaders can bridge generational divides and foster an environment where all team members feel valued and understood.

Moreover, leveraging the unique strengths of each generation can enhance teamwork and spur innovation. For example, the Silent Generation may offer extensive experience and wisdom that can benefit younger colleagues. Conversely, Generation Z brings modern insights, technological proficiency, and a fresh outlook to the table. By harnessing these varied strengths, organizations can create innovative solutions and achieve greater success.

To fully capitalize on generational diversity and harness its benefits, it is crucial to promote open communication and collaboration within teams. Initiatives such as mentorship programs, intergenerational training sessions, and team-building exercises can help bridge generational divides and cultivate a unified team environment that values each member's unique contributions. Recognizing and understanding the distinct perspectives and strengths of different generations is key to creating a supportive and dynamic workplace. By appreciating these diverse viewpoints, leaders can foster an inclusive atmosphere where all team members are empowered to excel. Ultimately, embracing generational differences enables organizations to unlock their workforce's full potential, driving both innovation and overall success.

Generational diversity in the workplace offers numerous advantages that can significantly boost team success. Combining various age groups, including Baby Boomers, Gen X, Millennials, and Gen Z, introduces a broad spectrum of perspectives, experiences, and skills. This blend fosters innovation and creative problem-solving as each generation contributes its unique insights and methods.

A major advantage of this diversity is the opportunity for cross-generational learning and knowledge sharing. Each age group brings its own set of experiences and expertise, allowing team members to benefit from perspectives they might not encounter otherwise. For instance, seasoned professionals can impart extensive industry knowledge and practical wisdom, while younger employees can offer modern viewpoints and advanced technological skills.

Furthermore, generational diversity promotes effective collaboration and teamwork. As team members from different generations interact, they develop a greater appreciation for each other's abilities and contributions. By harnessing these varied strengths, teams can enhance their overall productivity and performance, leading to more successful outcomes.

Moreover, diversity greatly enhances our shared human experience by weaving together a rich fabric of perspectives, cultures, and ideas that expand our understanding of the world. When people from diverse backgrounds collaborate, they bring distinct viewpoints influenced by their unique life experiences, facilitating a dynamic exchange of insights and creativity. This vibrant mix not only boosts problem-solving and innovation but also fosters empathy and broadens our global outlook. By valuing and celebrating our differences, we build a more inclusive and nuanced world where varied voices and experiences come together to propel progress and enrich our collective journey.

Creating a framework for fostering intergenerational harmony involves integrating insights from psychology, sociology, and practical examples from successful organizations. A comprehensive approach begins with understanding the psychological aspects of generational differences, such as communication styles, values, and motivations. For instance, as stated above, Baby Boomers often value loyalty and face-to-face communication, while Millennials may prioritize flexibility and digital interaction. Recognizing these preferences can help tailor strategies that bridge generational gaps, such as implementing flexible work policies that accommodate various communication styles and work preferences.

From a sociological perspective, building intergenerational harmony requires creating environments where different age groups can interact meaningfully and collaboratively. Sociological research highlights the benefits of mixed-age teams in promoting mutual understanding and respect. Successful organizations such as IBM and Procter & Gamble have demonstrated this by establishing mentoring programs and cross-generational team projects. These initiatives allow for knowledge exchange between older and younger employees, fostering an atmosphere where diverse experiences are valued and leveraged. By creating structured opportunities for different generations to work together, organizations can enhance collaboration and break down stereotypes.

Real-world success stories further illustrate effective strategies for fostering intergenerational harmony. For example, Google promotes a culture of inclusivity through mentorship and collaboration across age groups, which has been integral to their innovative success. Similarly, the retirement community Aegis Living uses a "multi-generational living" model where younger and older residents engage in various activities together, fostering mutual respect and learning. These examples show that when organizations and communities actively create spaces for intergenerational interaction and respect, they can harness the full potential of their diverse age groups, leading to increased innovation and overall success.

One compelling example of bridging generational gaps comes from the story of Pat and Charlie, a dynamic duo in a small-town bakery. Pat, a Baby Boomer, had spent decades perfecting traditional recipes and running the bakery with a focus on time-honored practices. Charlie, a Millennial with a passion for modern food trends and digital marketing, joined the bakery with innovative ideas for expanding their reach. By blending Pat's expertise with Charlie's fresh perspectives, they transformed the bakery into a local hotspot. Pat's classic recipes were paired with Charlie's social media campaigns and contemporary flavors, creating a vibrant fusion that attracted a diverse customer base. This collaboration not only revitalized the business but also demonstrated how generational synergy can lead to substantial and positive change.

In the corporate world, the story of Mary Barra, CEO of General Motors, exemplifies effective intergenerational bridging. Barra, a leader known for her inclusive approach, has fostered an environment where diverse generational perspectives are valued. She implemented initiatives such as reverse mentoring programs, where younger employees guide senior leaders on emerging technologies and trends. This approach has not only improved GM's innovation but also created a culture of mutual respect and learning. Under her leadership, GM has successfully navigated significant industry changes, including advancements in electric vehicles and autonomous driving, showcasing how embracing generational diversity can drive organizational success.

On a broader scale, the experience of the intergenerational mentorship program at the nonprofit organization Encore.org highlights the impact of bridging generational divides for social good. The program connects older adults with younger people to collaborate on community projects and social innovations. One notable partnership involved a retired engineer working with a young entrepreneur to develop a low-cost water purification system for developing countries. This collaboration combined the engineer's practical knowledge with the entrepreneur's innovative approach, resulting in a groundbreaking solution that addressed a critical global issue. The success of such initiatives underscores the transformative power of intergenerational cooperation in creating meaningful and lasting positive change.

Enhanced intergenerational understanding and cooperation have the potential to drive substantial global progress across various critical areas, including climate change, education, and the future of work. In addressing climate change, the collaboration between different age groups can harness the unique strengths of each generation. Younger generations, often more attuned to emerging technologies and sustainability practices, can work alongside older generations, who bring a wealth of experience and historical perspective on environmental issues. By combining their insights, innovative solutions for reducing carbon footprints, advancing renewable energy technologies, and implementing effective climate policies can be developed, creating a more unified and effective response to this global challenge.

In the realm of education, intergenerational cooperation offers a chance to reimagine learning experiences and bridge knowledge gaps. Older educators and industry veterans can share their deep expertise and real-world experiences with younger learners, while younger educators and students can introduce modern pedagogical techniques and digital tools. This cross-generational exchange can create more dynamic and adaptable educational systems that better prepare students for the complexities of the future. For example, integrating practical experience from retirees into curricula can provide students with valuable insights into various professions, while incorporating new technologies can make learning more engaging and relevant.

The future of work is another area poised for transformation through improved intergenerational collaboration. As the workforce becomes increasingly diverse in age, blending the traditional work ethic and expertise of older employees with the technological proficiency and innovative mindset of younger workers can lead to more efficient and creative work environments. Companies that embrace this diversity can benefit from a more adaptable and resilient workforce capable of navigating rapid changes and driving innovation. By fostering a culture of mutual respect and shared learning, organizations can better address the evolving demands of the global economy, leading to more effective solutions.

Reflecting on the profound benefits of intergenerational understanding and cooperation, it is clear that everyone has a role to play in becoming "generational bridge-builders." By actively seeking to connect with people from different age groups in their personal and professional lives, they can contribute to a more inclusive and harmonious society. Engage with colleagues, family members, and community groups across generations to share insights, learn from each other, and work collaboratively towards common goals. Whether it's through mentorship programs, cross-generational projects, or simple acts of empathy and respect, every effort counts in bridging the gaps between generations.

In the community, take the initiative to create or support programs that foster intergenerational interactions. This could involve organizing events that bring together different generational cohorts' shared activities, establishing local mentorship programs, or advocating for policies that promote inclusivity. By championing these initiatives, you help build stronger, more cohesive communities where diverse perspectives are valued and leveraged. The collective wisdom and innovation that emerge from such collaborations can drive significant positive change and contribute to solving pressing issues, from local challenges to global concerns.

Looking towards the future, people's commitment to building generational bridges can leave a lasting impact. As they work together to create a less divided world, they set the stage for a more collaborative and understanding society for generations to come. By fostering intergenerational harmony today, they lay the foundation for a world where future generations inherit a legacy of mutual respect and shared progress. Embrace the opportunity to be a generational bridge-builder and make a difference—The right actions today can create a more connected and compassionate world for tomorrow.

— Conclusion—

Each of the four generations—Silent Generation, Baby Boomers, Generation X, Millennials, and Generation Z—brings a distinct set of experiences and values shaped by the eras they grew up in. The Silent Generation, who came of age during the aftermath of World War II, witnessed a world defined by recovery and rebuilding. Their formative years were marked by a strong work ethic and a focus on stability. In contrast, the Baby Boomers enjoyed a period of economic prosperity and social change, capitalizing on booming industries and expanding opportunities. Their experiences led them to value hard work and upward mobility, often prioritizing career success and financial security.

Generation X, shaped by a more balanced approach to work and life, emerged in an era of shifting economic landscapes and evolving social norms. This generation sought to create a healthier work-life balance compared to their more work-focused predecessors, emphasizing the importance of personal time and family life. Growing up in the digital age, Millennials encountered a more challenging economic environment, marked by the Great Recession and rising student debt, which influenced their perspectives on job stability and technology. Today, Generation Z is redefining the future of work with their digital fluency, demand for inclusivity, and emphasis on flexibility and social responsibility. As this youngest generation enters the workforce, they are driving significant changes in workplace culture, advocating for remote work, diversity, and innovation. Each generation's unique experiences contribute to a richer understanding of how to navigate and improve our evolving world.

The ongoing debate about whether generational conflicts will ever subside continues to be a prominent issue, with evidence of both clashes and successful collaborations across different age groups. Historically, there have been instances where generational differences have led to friction but ultimately resulted in mutual understanding and innovative progress. However, recent social media trends have amplified these generational tensions, starkly highlighting the differing value systems between younger and older generations. This digital spotlight often accentuates the divide, underscoring the challenges and opportunities for bridging these gaps in today's interconnected world.

The dialogue between Baby Boomers and Millennials has often been marked by criticism from both sides. Baby Boomers, born between 1946 and 1965, frequently accuse Millennials of entitlement, claiming they seek undue recognition for minimal effort. On the other hand, Millennials, born between 1980 and 1996, argue that Boomers are disconnected from modern realities. They believe Boomers unfairly blame them for the decline of traditional industries, like cereal, due to Millennials' different spending habits, such as prioritizing savings and purchasing avocados. Millennials also feel that Boomers have jeopardized their future by hoarding wealth and dismantling vital social programs, while Boomers often view Millennials as overly focused on issues like student debt instead of pursuing hard work and employment.

Karl Mannheim's groundbreaking 1927 essay, "The Problem of Generations," offers valuable insight into how U.S. Millennials form a distinct political generation with unique experiences and viewpoints that differentiate them from previous cohorts of young activists. Often referred to as "digital natives," Millennials have been deeply shaped by the Internet and emerging technologies, enabling them to utilize network-based communication, particularly social media, with unprecedented scale and effectiveness. This generation has expressed frustration with older generations, criticizing them for perceived environmental damage and economic mismanagement. Faced with rising living costs and inflation, Millennials are forging new paths and holding those responsible for past injustices accountable, reflecting their distinct approach to addressing contemporary challenges.

On the other end, Gen Z's eagerness to embrace change and their forward-thinking approach are driving significant cultural and societal shifts. Building on the progress made by Millennials, they are using their unique skills and perspectives to foster a more inclusive, equitable, and dynamic society. Their confidence and proactive mindset position them as pivotal agents of change in the coming decades. According to a recent Pew Research Center survey, Millennials and Gen Z are notably more engaged with climate change than older generations. They are more vocal about the urgent need for climate action, frequently encounter climate-related content on social media, and actively participate in environmental causes through volunteering, rallies, and protests. This heightened awareness and activism underscore a generational shift towards more robust environmental advocacy.

Generation Alpha is set to be the most technologically proficient and digitally immersed generation yet. Growing up surrounded by smartphones, AI, and the Internet of Things, they will engage with a wide range of digital devices from an early age, likely exceeding the screen time of any previous generation. This deep integration with technology will profoundly influence their learning, communication, and entertainment, leading to new patterns of interaction and skill development. As they adapt to a world where digital connectivity is pervasive, their experiences will represent a vast social experiment, the full implications of which are still unfolding.

The ongoing discourse between Baby Boomers and Millennials often revolves around recurring criticisms, epitomized by the "OK Boomer" meme, which reflects Millennials' and Gen Z's frustration with older generations' perceived lack of understanding of their challenges. This generational tension can be analyzed through social science concepts like in-group bias and the fundamental attribution error.

In-group bias, studied by social psychologists like Henri Tajfel and John Turner, describes the tendency to favor one's own generation while viewing others less favorably. This bias can lead to negative stereotypes about different generations, as people often overlook the strengths of those outside their group and emphasize their flaws. The fundamental attribution error further exacerbates this issue by causing individuals to attribute negative behaviors of other generations to inherent traits rather than considering broader social and economic contexts. This psychological lens helps explain the criticisms exchanged between generations and highlights the complexity of intergenerational relationships.

Workplace expectations are evolving in response to broader generational shifts and changing attitudes toward employment. The rise of job-hopping reflects a move toward more dynamic and flexible work environments, requiring both employees and employers to adapt by embracing continuous learning and agile career paths.

The traditional 9-to-5 work model, which has dominated the American workforce for over a century, is being disrupted by technological advances, changing worker expectations, and new business demands. The gig economy, fueled by platforms like Uber, Airbnb, and various freelance websites, has expanded significantly, offering younger generations greater control over their work schedules and career paths. This shift enables them to select projects and set hours that align with their personal needs and preferences.

Cross-generational learning brings significant benefits by fostering a vibrant exchange of knowledge and perspectives that enhances older adults' cognitive experiences. When younger individuals introduce new concepts and technologies, it prompts older adults to think critically and adapt, boosting their cognitive flexibility and problem-solving skills. This interaction often results in increased self-esteem and a sense of purpose, which supports cognitive health. A study in JAMA Network Open (2020) found that older adults engaged in activities and with younger people experienced improved memory and cognitive function, underscoring the positive impact of such exchanges on mental well-being.

Additionally, generational diversity enhances teamwork and collaboration. Interactions between team members from different generations foster mutual appreciation of each other's skills and contributions. By leveraging these diverse strengths, teams can improve productivity and achieve more successful outcomes.

This evolving perspective is prompting employers to rethink work arrangements to attract and retain top talent from younger generations. Flexible schedules and remote work options are increasingly favored by Gen Z, making companies that offer these benefits more attractive. Organizations that adapt to these preferences can better engage and motivate their workforce.

Globalization and the pandemic have further shifted workforce norms, making the traditional workday less relevant. Workers now prioritize roles that offer personal fulfillment and recognition over conventional job functions. Many modern companies are designing work environments that leverage the strengths of all generations, understanding the value of a diverse workforce. Firms like IBM are leading the way with flexible schedules, remote work options, and continuous development opportunities to support a multi-generational team.

AI is expected to bring both challenges and opportunities to the job market. Future careers will require adaptability, continuous learning, and a rethinking of work structures and values. This means preparing for a constantly evolving work environment for younger and future generations, focusing on skills that enhance and complement human capabilities alongside technological advancements.

Intergenerational teamwork has proven effective in social justice, as seen in the climate movement. Experienced environmentalists are now collaborating with passionate young activists like Greta Thunberg, combining historical insight with fresh perspectives. This synergy has fueled impactful global initiatives like Fridays for Future and important policy debates. To bridge generational value gaps while respecting differing beliefs, strategic communication is essential. By highlighting shared goals, such as improving job satisfaction and productivity, companies can align diverse values and achieve mutual success.

Both older and younger generations should actively work to understand each other's communication styles. For example, when older individuals learn modern slang like "FOMO" or "drip," it helps them connect better with younger generations, showing respect for their perspectives and fostering more engaging conversations.

When younger people take an interest in the slang of older generations, such as "threads" for style or "groovy" for something exciting, it shows respect and a willingness to connect. This mutual effort enhances understanding and enriches conversations. Families often bridge these gaps by using shared communication tools like WhatsApp or Snapchat, where younger members teach older ones to use technology and vice versa, strengthening bonds and improving interactions.

Imagine a world where generational tensions are seen as opportunities for growth rather than sources of conflict. By fostering open dialogue and mutual respect, these tensions can become valuable learning experiences that strengthen familial bonds and create a more empathetic society.

Embracing and working through these challenges can lead to more resilient relationships and a deeper understanding among all generations.

In recent years, reverse mentoring has emerged as a dynamic tool for both personal and professional development, challenging the traditional model where knowledge flows solely from senior to junior employees. This approach, gaining traction since the late 1990s, highlights the value of knowledge exchange across different generational levels.

With Generation Z joining the workforce, today's workplaces are a blend of four distinct generations, each bringing its unique experiences and perspectives. Reverse mentoring stands out as a powerful method, offering fresh learning and knowledge exchange opportunities that traditional mentoring may overlook. This approach not only values the contributions of junior employees but also ensures that senior staff stay informed about current social and technological trends, enriching the organization overall.

Looking ahead, the effort to build bridges between generations can create a lasting impact. By working together to foster a more unified and cooperative society, people pave the way for future generations to thrive in an environment of mutual respect and collaboration. Today's commitment to intergenerational harmony sets the groundwork for a future where respect and shared progress are the legacy passed on to the next generations.

References.

Mannheim, K. (1927). The problem of generations (P. Kecskemeti, Trans.).Retrieved from https://marcuse.faculty.history.ucsb.edu classes/201/articles/27MannheimGenerations.pdf

Generation Empathy: The Surprising Surge of Compassion in Modern Youth | SPSP. (2024, July 26). https://spsp.org/news/character-and-context blog/martingano-modern-youth-compassion-empathy-increase

www.ingramcontent.com/pod-product-compliance
Lightning Source LLC
Chambersburg PA
CBHW051216120626
46547CB00013B/1377